*When All the Laughter
Died in Sorrow*

When All the Laughter Died in Sorrow

LANCE RENTZEL

Saturday Review Press

NEW YORK

The title of this book, *When All the Laughter Died in Sorrow*, is from the poem by Kendrew Lascelles.

Published simultaneously in Canada by
Doubleday Canada Ltd., Toronto.

Library of Congress Catalog Card Number: 72-79037

ISBN 0-8415-0208-0

Saturday Review Press
230 Park Avenue
New York, New York 10017

Printed in the United States of America

Design by Tere LoPrete

THIS BOOK IS DEDICATED TO:

My family
My teammates
And Joey

When All the Laughter
Died in Sorrow

I

Monday, November 23, 1970, ten o'clock in the morning. Officer Williams, a member of the Dallas Police Force, arrived at the front door of my parents' house. He rang the bell and Bernice, the lady who worked for Mom, answered. The policeman was polite, a friendly guy. He'd been around a few times to talk football; a Cowboy fan. He explained that he had gone over to my apartment and hadn't found me and asked if I was there. Bernice said that I had stayed over for the night and was upstairs sleeping, but was it anything special? "Well," he said, "not really, but when he wakes up, would you ask him to drop over to the station?"

My mother heard. She was in the bathroom, just finishing washing her hair, a towel turbaned over her head, but she heard. Like all other concerned mothers, when something came up about any of her children she had ears that bent around corners.

"What is it, Bernice?" she called out; but she didn't wait for an answer, she was already on her way to the door.

Officer Williams smiled in greeting, hat in hand.

"Good morning, Mrs. Rentzel."

He was smiling, yes, but my mother could see right through it. It wasn't a happy smile, not like his usual happy-to-be-here smile. She had a premonition of pain, but told herself that she really had no reason to be afraid, that she tended to overreact.

"Oh, good morning, Officer Williams." She smiled back.

The officer was uncomfortable as he pulled out his notebook. My mother blanched.

"This Thunderbird . . . license number . . . does it belong to Lance?"

"Yes. It's on loan to him from one of the Ford agencies in town."

Williams smiled. "Well, when he wakes up, would you ask him to drop by the station?"

"Certainly, but what's it all about?"

He hesitated, then looked around the foyer like a man who was terribly uncomfortable about what he had to say. He took my mother gently by the arm and led her into the living room, and they both sat down, on the edge of their soft-cushioned seats. The policeman's voice was soft, barely audible; he obviously did not wish Bernice or anyone else to hear.

"A man who was driving that Thunderbird, Mrs. Rentzel, last Thursday afternoon, he stopped the car and, well, he supposedly exposed himself to a little girl. . . ."

My mother smiled, trying to indicate how silly this all was. She swallowed once, that was all, just one quick swallow. She told herself, well, that was what it was, obviously an error, a different Thunderbird surely, or perhaps someone else was driving it, or it was some silly joke that one of my kooky friends had drummed up. Her son Lance, the better-than-perfect Lance, the all-American hero, happily married to that marvelous little Joey Heatherton Rentzel, it could never be Lance who would ever dream of doing a thing like that.

"Wait here, Officer—I'll go wake him up."

Williams was very uncomfortable. No, he really didn't care to wait, he even rose to leave, he felt he had done his duty, indeed, he had done more than that.

"Please," my mother insisted. She, too, was on her feet, halfway out of the room. "I'll get him."

I was sleeping, dreaming lovely dreams. There was something painfully significant about that. I was about to be in the worst trouble in my life and I was dreaming blissfully away. We had beaten the Redskins badly the day before. I had had a good day. Nothing spectacular, but good. I played a good game: caught five passes, blocked well, hit hard. The mood during the flight back to Dallas was light and full of fun. We were having a bad season, but it's the nature of football teams to respond most to their last game. I'd gone to a party with my friends that night. I'd had a good time. And though I missed Joey, who was appearing at Caesar's Palace in Las Vegas, I would see her in a few days, after the Thanksgiving Day game. I'd have the whole weekend with her in Vegas. I was dreaming about that.

Then I heard my mother's voice: "Lance . . . Lance . . ."

I opened my eyes to daylight and immediately checked the time out of some familiar feeling that it was late and that she was calling to get me up in time for our one o'clock practice. It was only ten o'clock.

5

"What is it?" I mumbled.

She opened the door and came into the room. She sat down on the side of the big bed, fussing with the towel on her hair.

"There's a policeman downstairs, you remember him, Officer Williams. . . . He wants to see you."

End of dream, beginning of horror.

"What does he want?" I asked—as if I didn't know.

"Something about indecent exposure. . . ."

I am six foot two and I weigh 200 pounds and I've been hit by 250-pound linebackers with the power of a two-and-a-half-ton truck. It is nothing compared to the impact of those few words. I felt a terrible fear. My head began to spin and a cold sweat broke out all over me.

"He said you don't have to get up now," my mother said. "You could drop over later. . . ."

"No, I'll get up."

My mother nodded approvingly, smiling again as though she weren't worried; therefore there was no reason for me to worry, right?

Wrong.

I got dressed and the fear dwindled, replaced by speculations. I wondered what might happen, trying to figure out an approach, but my mind kept referring to the past. I'd been in this exact spot before. In 1966, when I was playing for the Minnesota Vikings, I was at practice, and it wasn't my mother, it was Coach Norm Van Brocklin who broke the news. He brought me into his office, trying to figure me out. It was one of the few times I ever saw him ill at ease. He said to me, apologetically, "I hate to ask you this, but did you expose yourself to two small girls?"

The same thing this time: the police had traced my license plates. Somebody had seen it happen and taken down the number.

Officer Williams was in the living room, waiting for me, and he stood up when he saw me.

"Hi, Mr. Rentzel," he said. He called me *Mr.* Rentzel. "I know this is ridiculous, this business, but I've been asked to tell you to come down to the station some time today."

"I'll come with you now," I said.

He was uneasy at that, as though he wanted me to have breakfast first or something like that. Actually, I seldom eat breakfast. Besides, if I did, I wouldn't have been able to eat on that morning.

"Well, you can drop in later, you know," he repeated.

"This business, Mr. Rentzel, I'm sure it's not true."

I nodded. There it was again, opening the door to the dream world. This was Lance Rentzel and he could not possibly do a thing like that.

I put on my jacket and said good-bye to my mother. I got in my Thunderbird to follow Officer Williams to the station, and after three blocks my car died. Out of gas.

I guess that has happened at some time or another to everyone who has ever driven a car, but this time it really bothered me, as if I were heading for trouble and everything was going to come down on me at once.

The policeman stopped his car, turned around, and came back for me. I saw window curtains parting on all sides, and women standing in doorways. I saw cars slow down and stop to look. I saw them all, and as I got into the squad car my ears were buzzing with the distant babble of voices.

Johnny Cash used to sing a song about moments like this: "Bad news travels like wildfire, good news travels slow." The gossip had already started.

The police station was a clean-looking old English-style building in the middle of a beautiful park. It was a bright, sunny day, with blue sky and lots of white clouds. A perfect day to be arrested.

Inside, Chief Forrest Keene was sitting at his desk,

7

fumbling through papers. He looked up at me as if to be sure it was really Lance Rentzel standing there with his head about to crack open. And then he started to read aloud.

It was a short paragraph or so, charging that on Thursday, November 19, 1970, at 4:15 P.M., a male Caucasian in a black Thunderbird had driven up to a curb in University Park, beckoned a ten-year-old girl toward the car by asking for directions, exposed himself to her, and then driven away. He read it in such a cold, matter-of-fact way that the charge might have been anything from double-parking to multiple homicide.

When he finished, my instincts were all for self-preservation, so I kept silent. I knew from his tone and his looks that it was going to be a really serious business this time, much worse than what happened in Minnesota. This was going to be more than my just coming down to the station to talk about it.

"The man who made the charges—it was his little girl who witnessed the exposure—well, he's very upset about it. He seems rather sure of himself, that it was you who did it."

"I'd like to talk to this gentleman," I said. I guess I'm pretty adept at talking my way out of trouble. And though I don't really know for sure what to say at a moment like this, I thought I could work my way through such a confrontation if I had to. I can think on my feet, as they say.

"He doesn't want to talk to you," the chief said.

I nodded, trying to keep my composure. The other policemen were all being very nice. I asked Chief Keene, "May I make a phone call?"

I called Carl Oates, a Dallas lawyer who is a good friend of mine. I told him where I was, and he said he'd be right over, and that I should call Tex Schramm, general manager of the Cowboys. I called Tex and he came over too, with Bob Thompson, a minority owner of the club. They were all there in minutes, and I felt a tremendous sense of relief: like a drowning man with a couple of great swimmers coming to save him. They assured Chief Forrest Keene that they were eager to cooperate with everyone, to do nothing but help the police in this matter, and to get the police to cooperate with us so that this affair could be handled in a way that nobody got hurt. The chief agreed with that. He didn't want to see anyone hurt either.

Above all, it was vital that it be kept quiet. The worst thing would be if the press got wind of it. They'd have a field day with Lance Rentzel.

Again the police agreed. There was, however, a big problem: the man who had filed the charges, the father of the little girl, was an attorney named Paul Adams, a very reputable, responsible man with a prominent Dallas law firm.

My lifesavers were not bothered by that. They began their rescue campaign by trying to get Paul Adams to drop the charges. I realized immediately that it was Paul Adams who held the key to my fate.

So it ended on a promising note. I was technically under arrest, but free to go. Chief Keene was very nice, I could feel his sympathy and concern. In no way did he give us the feeling that he was out to get me.

I got to practice about an hour late and told Coach Tom Landry that I had been with Tex Schramm, who would call and explain later.

The practice session itself was so strange, it fed the weird, dreamlike quality of the day. The Cowboys were down; though not mathematically out of the race, we certainly were psychologically. For the first time, Coach

Landry decided to ease up and let practice be a thing of pleasure. We were going to play Green Bay on Thursday, Thanksgiving Day, but that day the name of the game was touch football, an unheard-of action at a Landry practice session. Lots of mad, wild fleaflicker plays: everything from triple and quadruple reverses to Statues of Liberty and crazy behind-the-back laterals. Defensive linemen were the new quarterbacks. Eerie sound effects of hilarious laughter. Sheer unadulterated schoolboy fun. Even Landry, that marvelously square, serious man, was laughing. Some were saying that he was through as a coach, that he was going to be retired, that he had gone to bat too many times with this great club and had struck out. Criticism of the team had reached an all-time high. The press, especially in New York, was showing nothing but disgust for our failures. We were everybody's cop-outs, the greatest choke-up team in history. But in the bright sunlight of a crisp November afternoon there was nothing but joy for the club, forty friendly guys deserted by the experts, deserted by their fans, suddenly welded together by the scorn of the world, a team with nothing more to lose and everything to gain.

Except for Lance Rentzel.

I laughed, too, but it was all part of my dream. I was not really there. This wasn't the Cowboys playing touch football. It couldn't be. And that couldn't be Coach Tom Landry laughing with his third-place team. A dream, yes. The whole day was a dream, a terrible dream. The worst feeling I will ever know is to have to put on a front when you think you're going to die.

The touch football game ended, and I called home to tell Mom not to worry. (Don't worry, Mom, your wonderful son is just a sex pervert.) There were players standing around the telephone booth, so I could tell her nothing else, except to ask her if she would pick up my car for me, and that I'd be by to see her shortly.

10

Mother: Lance followed the policeman to the station that Monday morning. I did not hear anything all day, and I was frantic with worry. I knew the papers would pick up the fact that he had been questioned—there'd be a rehash of Minnesota—and the publicity would destroy him; but still I never doubted his innocence. . . . Never once did it occur to me that this was anything but a frame-up. He called me about three from the training room to tell me that his car had run out of gas. Later I learned that when Officer Williams gave Lance a ride to the station he didn't advise him of his civil rights at any time during the ride. And going to the station in the squad car meant that he was technically under arrest. This was a clear-cut violation of his civil rights—the first of many to follow. I am convinced that civil rights are only for racial minorities and mass murderers.

We had a little difficulty locating my father in Washington to tell him what had happened. When we finally got through to him, he was understandably upset and immediately left for Dallas.

It is scary the way news leaks. Nothing can possibly happen around a police station without some reporter hearing about it. By that same evening the word was already out. Joey's brother, Dickie Heatherton, a disc jockey at KLIF, a station in Dallas, had heard about it. He called me at home to tell me, and I wondered if it was all going to break into the open even before Carl Oates and the Cowboy management got a chance to resolve the legal situation with Paul Adams and the police.

Finally I reached Joey in Las Vegas. I had spent the long

day waiting to speak to her, but I knew it was not going to be easy. I wanted her to know the truth, every bit of it, but I didn't want her to suffer. When I heard her voice, finally, I just cracked up. "I'm in trouble," I told her, and I fell apart. She sensed immediately what was wrong. I don't know how, but she did. I had told her about Minnesota a long time ago, before we were married, and she listened to it all but never said anything about it. We never mentioned the subject again. Now I let out all my emotions, wanting to be with her so much, and she was very understanding. She was everything I needed at that moment. She even said she'd cut short her nightclub engagement to be with me in Dallas. I told her that wasn't necessary, since I'd be in Vegas in three days.

I began to ride with hope. On Tuesday things began to look more promising. Carl Oates spoke to Paul Adams, the father of the little girl, and his report was not foreboding. Apparently Adams had no doubt that it was me. His daughter had told him what had happened, remembering the black car and my long blond hair. Another friend of his had remembered that I drove such a car, so he went by my parents' home during that weekend, when the Cowboys were in Washington, and saw it parked in the driveway. Then on that Sunday, during the televising of the game, his daughter saw a shaving cream commercial I'd made and she said, Yes, that's him! It was on Monday, then, that he filed a complaint with the police.

Not that I blamed the girl's parents for their attitude. I guess I would be outraged if I had a daughter and a man exposed himself to her. Maybe I would press charges too. I felt deeply ashamed of what I had done. I realized the mental harm I could have possibly inflicted on the girl. I sincerely wished I could speak with her parents to make it up to them in some way, but they still refused to talk to me.

12

Carl Oates: I asked him [Paul Adams] what his intentions were with regard to the complaint, and he said that he had no vindictive motives and was not vengeful, he merely felt that he was not going to obstruct whatever course the law took. If that involved a lineup or hearing or trial, whatever, they were prepared to go ahead. He had talked it over with his little girl and asked her what she wanted to do. Her response was that it was not what she wanted to do but what she thought was right to do—that if someone commits a crime and you know about it, you should press to see that they are punished for the crime. . . .

This had to be handled quietly. For example, a regular police lineup for identification would be disastrous, even though there was always a chance that the little Adams girl might not be able to identify me and the whole case against me would then fall apart. There were even some people who claimed that I really ought to counterattack, to claim complete innocence, to deny everything, to place the entire burden of proof on them. But this was inadvisable from a practical standpoint. There would be too much publicity at such a trial. And even if I managed to win the case, I'd end up the loser. Obviously I was not just an ordinary citizen anymore. I was a celebrity, a colorful type whom the press loved to write about. Furthermore, I was married to a celebrity. One could easily picture the fun the media would have with me.

No, my best chance was to settle this thing as quietly as possible. Chief Keene explained that a lineup was not necessary, that a statement from me would satisfy the law, a statement to the effect that I was there, riding in the neighborhood of University Park on that Thursday afternoon. It was not a confession of guilt. It merely admitted my presence.

> *Mother: This was the first thing that embittered me, because later we learned that the description Adams gave did not fit Lance. They described a man with long hair and muttonchop sideburns—and Lance's hair at that time was fairly short and he has never worn sideburns that could in any way be described as "muttonchop." Had it not been for this written statement, Lance could have gone to trial—and wouldn't have had to take whatever Mr. Adams dished out. . . .*

Meanwhile my friends were lining up behind me. Bob Strauss, a lawyer in Dallas and head of the Democratic National Committee, returned from Washington and met with Carl, Tex, and Clint Murchison, owner of the Cowboys. Bob went to work to keep the press from exploiting this matter, warning it that since charges had not been filed against me, it would be ill-advised to publish anything that might prejudice my position. There were further meetings with the Cowboys on whether or not I should play on Thursday. It was a touchy problem. Might that not arouse whatever resentment Paul Adams must already have felt and spur him to press charges? But then, if I didn't play, what reason could be given to the media? Since rumors were already rampant, wouldn't this create even greater suspicion?

14

That afternoon, Tuesday, Coach Landry came up to me in practice, having heard the details from Tex Schramm.

"I'm sorry this has happened, Lance. I hope it can be kept out of the papers so you can play. Is that what you want to do?"

"I'd like to continue playing, yes."

It was decided that I should keep on as usual, practice and play—which was exactly what I wanted to do.

I heard from Dickie Heatherton again that night. He told me that there was a great debate going on among the press people, some demanding that the story be released, and others wanting to hold back, fearing a possible libel suit. I could only hope that they would hold off until the matter had a chance to be resolved in my favor.

Hope, yes. I was hoping. I was hoping that somehow I could come away from this without being destroyed. I was scratching and clawing to survive, I could hardly think of anything else, nobody talked of anything else, every phone call I made, every meeting I had, every thought was directed toward it.

Two ironies about the case had a touch of Hitchcock to them. Mr. Adams told Carl that about a year before the incident he had sat next to Joey on a flight from New York to Dallas. He had shown her pictures of his wife and children and had enjoyed a pleasant conversation with her. When they got off the plane, I was waiting for Joey and she introduced him to me. We talked for a moment, then went our separate ways, never dreaming that our paths would cross again.

The other oddity involved our schnauzer, Scarlett O'Hara. Shortly after my arrest, the dog disappeared. Mom searched for blocks and finally found her romping around the lawn of the Adamses' house with their dog. This was to happen several more times.

It was obvious by Wednesday that my teammates had

15

heard the rumors. No one came out and said anything, but I could sense they were looking at me strangely. I didn't know whether to say anything or not. Bob Strauss called to tell me that the Dallas papers had agreed to hold off printing anything, that the situation was, as he put it, "85 percent under control." I was relieved, at least for the moment.

Then I got a call telling me that the *Oklahoma City Times*—from the town where my family was prominent, and where I grew up—had plastered the whole story all over the front page, and there was a good chance that it might be picked up by the wire services and released across the entire country.

That night I knew what I had to do. There was a team meeting at the Hilton Hotel, where we stayed before our home games. About fifty of us were crowded into the meeting room. Some were standing because there weren't enough chairs for us all. Landry walked in and opened the meeting. He told the team that I had something I wanted to say. . . .

Because of the confined space, everyone seemed almost on top of me, and all I could feel was a sudden burst of shame. In a sense, I had never really been one of them. Mostly I lived a different way of life from theirs. Different kinds of friends, different backgrounds. I dressed differently, wore my hair longer, acted less conservatively than most. When I was single, I avoided the parties of the married crowd and went my own way, because I felt a little out of place. After I married Joey, I still stayed away because a couple of the other wives had not been friendly to her. Now I was going to ask them to bear with me, and I wondered if they would accept such a plea.

"I suppose you've all heard a lot of stories about me in the last few days, and I feel you should hear from me what's going on. Well, the stories are pretty much true, and

I want you to understand the truth about it, so that you'll know how to handle it. . . . I guess everybody makes mistakes in his life. Well, I've made some bad ones. I'm in serious trouble and I don't know what's going to happen."

I got that much out without too much difficulty; then I began to choke badly. But for the first time they were seeing the real me. They were witnessing emotions that I really felt, but rarely expressed. It was not a prepared speech, I was just speaking from the heart; a few minutes, that's all I wanted to take, but it got so I was not sure I could finish.

"I want to apologize to you. If I've embarrassed you as teammates, I'm really sorry. I hope that you'll want me to stay on the team, and that you'll support me and consider me a friend—because that's what I want to be. That's what I want above all."

I sat down and there was not a sound for a second or two, then a few loud swallows, including my own. I sat there with my head down, feeling too ashamed to look at anyone. I wanted to crawl away and hide; I wanted this to be over. I was twenty-seven years old and I was supposed to be a responsible person. I was supposed to be a man with ambitions and big dreams, and all of a sudden I was a miserable idiot with a tremendous contempt for himself.

I started to cry, I couldn't help it, I fought it, holding my hand in front of my mouth. I looked up and saw that I wasn't the only one in tears. I wanted to run from the room, I began wishing Landry would turn out the damn lights and start the film so I could hide in the darkness, and it seemed like forever before they did.

Then, in the dark, Landry tried to bring everyone's attention back to the game, to watch the Green Bay kicking teams on film, but you could feel how impossible that was, I'd ruined that for the moment at least. Then this incredible thing happened: a hand grabbed my shoulder, a huge hand, and it held on, firmly, supportively, and then, from the other side, a tap on the arm, then again. The room was dark and the coach was talking, but there was a shuffling and a sound of scraping chairs, as one after another they moved to make contact with me. They wanted to remain anonymous and did not wish to be open about it, but they wanted to convey the unspoken message: "We're with you." I wondered how I could have doubted them. I knew one thing: I'd never forget that moment.

The meeting ended and the team went to dinner. The guys at my table talked normally, as they always did the night before a game. At times I forgot the trouble I was in and talked as if nothing had happened. Dan Reeves came up and whispered, "Everyone makes a mistake, but few people have the courage to stand up and admit it the way you did. We're all on your side." During the rest of the meal, other players and coaches approached me; each came alone and said something in his own way to let me know he was not judging me. They understood what I was going through and they felt for me. And now, for the first time, these men who hardly ever weaken or display their feelings were saying things they ordinarily wouldn't. It was interesting noticing who spoke to me and who didn't, although 1 realized that the ones who remained silent were not necessarily against me. Everyone reacts differently in a moment like this.

We were through at seven and had to be in our hotel rooms by eleven. I went home and ate an early Thanksgiving dinner with my family and relatives, but it was kind of a strain. I tried to enjoy myself as much as possible, but they all looked so sad, as if they were ready to cry. It was bearing on their shoulders as heavily as it was on mine. Whenever anything was mentioned about my case, it was done matter-of-factly, without emotion, or we might all have broken down. The only thing discussed was what my chances were of having the charges dropped.

At the dinner table, Mother said we still had a lot to be thankful for. I thought about how I had never really appreciated all that I had in life: a family and friends who cared for me; good enough athletic ability to be well paid for doing something that I enjoyed; enough intelligence and education to be able to succeed in a variety of other fields; good health, and most of all, a wonderful wife whom I loved very deeply. Now I faced prison, my reputation and career seemed down the drain, my political ambitions ruined, and my marriage bound to be affected by the scandal.

Thanksgiving Day was chilly, sunny, and windy. The Cotton Bowl filled up early, surprisingly so. We were warming up before the game, and I was trying to pull myself together. My body was where I wanted it to be, but my head was still weaving around police stations, press-rooms, lawyers' meetings. I concentrated on football as much as I could, knowing I had to do a good job, I had to repay the team for their support. We were running pass routes: a square out this time, and I cut to the sidelines. Craig Morton overthrew me, and the ball bounded over to the grandstand, into the hands of a young teen-age girl. I stood there looking at her, my hands outstretched in a gesture for its return; she seemed embarrassed, and as she finally threw it back at me, a big voice bellowed from several rows back, "That's the way, Rentzel, always playing with little girls."

I'll never forget that voice either. It was the first of a thousand abusive catcalls that would be directed at me in the months to come.

We played fine defense and held Green Bay without a

touchdown, winning 16-3. I wasn't thrown to very much, but I made a number of crucial plays as a runner and blocker, and I felt my teammates were proud of the way I played under all that pressure. We'd won our last two games and were climbing in the league standings. There was a fresh sense of team pride and pleasure in the locker room and everyone was feeling just fine.

And as for me, I was emotionally detached. I was listening to the friendly, supportive chatter of teammates when Tex Schramm told me that the wire services were not going to pick up the release from Oklahoma. He was even encouraged about the possibility of working things out with Paul Adams so that charges would not be pressed.

Yes, I was all right. I was better than all right. I was rushing to get dressed to get to the airport. I was on my way to Vegas to see Joey, and what could possibly be better than that? Some other Lance Rentzel was in trouble, not me.

Mother: *We waited for him at the dressing room to take him to the plane for Las Vegas. It took him forty-five minutes to get the fifty feet from the door to where we were standing, inching his way through the fans clamoring for his autograph. When the police finally helped him through the crush, and we were almost at the car, he saw a crippled little boy in a wheelchair forlornly holding out his program, and Lance went back and signed it, even talked to him for a moment—and was immediately engulfed by the crowd again. He would have missed the plane had it not been late. That is my son— what· he's always been, what he always will be.*

Joey was everything my troubled soul could hope for. We talked until she had to do her show. Her act was tremendous and, as always, I was thrilled by it. And when she was through, we went to see Frank Sinatra, Jr.'s show. We ended up in his room ordering dinner, and it turned into a big feast with all the trimmings. He showed us the TV special he'd made, with Sammy Davis, Jr., Dean Martin, and his father, and we all enjoyed it. For the next two days, Joey and I stayed in our room almost the entire time, satisfying my need to be alone with her. She was not threatened by my mysterious hang-ups, or hurt by them, because she knew it had nothing to do with her. She was sympathetic and loving, and I found great comfort in her presence.

On Saturday night I got a call from my mother, and Joey was no longer able to comfort me.

Mother: *All week the Adamses were pressuring the chief of police to charge Lance. Bob Strauss called us on Friday night and said he had spent two hours with Mr. Adams, and that since so many civic leaders and prominent citizens had called him trying to persuade him not to press charges, Mr. Adams had become impressed with his own power. Bob told him that it did not matter whether Lance was guilty or innocent, that the minute he filed charges, the publicity would destroy Lance and his family with him. Bob also said that Lance would go to any psychiatrist of Adams' choosing and as frequently as he wished. But he rejected the suggestion. There was no reasoning with him. This was his moment of glory. At the door Bob said to him, "Mr. Adams, you*

21

have five children. There's no way you can raise them in these troubled times without one or more of them getting into some sort of trouble. The day will come when you will ask for the mercy that you deny the Rentzel family."

Bob Strauss called me the next morning with a replay of my mother's news: it was looking bad with Paul Adams, and in all probability charges would be filed against me on Monday morning. Had too much pressure been put on Adams by the important people acting in my behalf? Or were the neighbors, most of whom were against me, influencing him and his wife? Perhaps Mrs. Adams was the reason. Chief Keene had met with them both several days before, and he told Carl that she was definitely the more adamant of the two. But it was useless to speculate, and I was resigned to the grim possibilities. I started packing my bag a day earlier than I'd planned, explaining to Joey that I had to go back and face the music. Inside, I knew that the ax was about to fall.

When I got back to Dallas, Carl told me that Adams had nothing more to say at the time, and all I could do was wait. It wasn't easy. I felt as if I were waiting for my own execution, but by this time I was resigned to it.

On Monday morning I had my first session with the psychiatrist who was to help me on my case. He was a distinguished man in his fifties, very intelligent and scholarly-looking, with glasses and a balding head. We chatted for an hour, getting acquainted, saving the serious problems for future meetings. We both knew that, at least in the beginning, his functions would be more legal than therapeutic. He would guide me into a deeper analysis of my problems later.

When I got to Carl Oates's office, Bob Strauss was there

to give me the bad news: charges had been filed that morning, the publicity was already out, clattering off press wires throughout the country, and I was a doomed man.

The big meeting took place later at Bob's office. Everybody was there, all the important people involved: club officials, coach, lawyers, parents, brothers, me—all to discuss what I should do. I was worried that I might have to retire. The thought of leaving football made my heart sink, but I could no longer think primarily of myself. It was better for the team that I shoulder this burden alone. They had enough to worry about.

Tex Schramm had a better idea: I could put myself on the move list, an inactive status, for a minimum of two weeks. The rules allowed me to practice and continue working out with the club, but not suit up for the games. In my case, it was considered best for everyone concerned if I didn't show up at all. But if everything went well legally, I could return in time for the play-offs, if the Cowboys went that far.

I could understand this. What with all the tremendous publicity surrounding the affair, most of it negative, it would seem to simplify everybody's life if I just got out of sight. As much as I wanted to play, I couldn't.

Tom Landry left to tell the team of my decision, and Tex and I drafted a statement for the press. Then I went to my apartment and tried to relax.

The news that evening was overwhelming. Every newspaper in America played it up, and it was on television coast to coast. Several sportscasters in New York said I no longer belonged in the world of sports. Walter Cronkite of CBS devoted a good deal of time to the story in his national news broadcast. In every instance, the incident in Minnesota was mentioned. Moreover, my wife was frequently referred to in the reports and was often pictured with me.

23

It was only the beginning. Whatever happened from here on in, this flurry of international publicity (carried by the wire services all the way to Japan, Australia, and Vietnam) was just the start of my problems. I knew wherever I went, or whatever I did, I was a marked man from this day on.

My phone never stopped ringing. I got calls from everywhere, all of them offering support, but the one I appreciated the most was from Craig Morton. "We'll see you at 9:30 in the morning," he said, "in time for practice." For the team had voted unanimously to ask me to continue playing. I was completely surprised by this. Once again, I realized how much these guys meant to me. They were willing to share my guilt in order to help me out. I knew how much I wanted to play, how much I *needed* to play, especially now when all the world was caving in on me, when my mind was going to be burdened with too many pressures, when my life threatened to become rootless and ridden with shame. If I could play ball, if I could be part of this team, if I could spend at least part of my day driving my body and my concentration toward this new Cowboy surge to the championship, everything else would be that much more tolerable. There was no legal or NFL rule to prevent me from playing. The team wanted me back, and I needed to go back. When Bob Hayes stopped in to chat—he had tried to call but couldn't get through—I told him, yes, I'd be there in the morning.

Hayes was a good friend, and what were good friends for but to go to jail with you when you had to post bond. It had been decided that night was a better time than day on what turned out to be a naïve belief that most of the press and TV people could be avoided. On the way downtown, we stopped at the office of my new criminal lawyer, Phil Burleson (indecent exposure to a girl under sixteen is a felony in Texas, punishable by imprisonment for up to fifteen years!), and the three of us then headed for the county courthouse.

24

Phil knew the rear entrance to the county jail, by which we avoided running into any reporters. When we got off the freight elevator on the fifth floor, the first thing I saw was the prison bars. It was then that the full impact of what I had done hit me. The prospect of prison was a shattering realization. A cold wind passed through me as the jailer clanked the door behind me, separating me from my lawyer and my friend. I saw the drunk tank, half filled with guys drying out for the night, and I couldn't help thinking that they were better off than I was. I was shuttled from desk to desk: papers to be filled out, questions to be answered, fingerprinting, mug shots. I tried to keep my dignity intact, but I must have looked like a broken man.

To make matters worse, the reporters had found out that I'd gotten by them, and they were furious. They demanded my appearance. The sheriff told me the bad news: I had to comply with the usual routine and meet them on the way out. A hero's welcome for the pride of Dallas. A dozen cameras loaded and ready to pop. Another dozen microphones thrust into my face. The TV cameras with the big glass eye that bored right through you. And questions, questions, a hundred questions all at once, I could hardly hear them, I wanted to die.

A hand on my arm guided me to the elevator. It was Phil Burleson and Bob Hayes. The cameras and questions followed me, police holding them back right at the closing elevator door. We went down to the parking level, and there they were again, they had beaten us down five flights, they followed me to the door, more questions, more pictures, swimming around me like wasps, so many now I couldn't move, we had to push through a human wall of clamoring voices and popping flashbulbs and a hundred eerie faces who were there for what, the last public look at an athlete who died young? I was shuddering again, my body was tense, and my mind had no sense of its reality, none at all, I could hear and see only blurs, all dreamlike again, yes, it was all a fantasy, a grotesque fantasy that had turned into a nightmare. I prayed to wake up and find that none of it had ever happened.

"Easy, man . . . easy," said Bob, his hand squeezing my arm.

The humiliation crushed me. I was being treated like a guilty man. Nobody was even assuming I might be innocent. Guilty though I was, I thought later that it was a terrible thing that the press could do to a man: innocent or guilty, all get painted by that same brush. Once they got on you, you were doomed, and there was no way you could clear your name, they dug your grave for you. They knew exactly what to say, they picked the words carefully, loading their stories with as much sensationalism as they could, either with outright accusations or simple innuendo. They were pros at it, and there was no way to stop them.

Yes, I was guilty—but not legally so, not yet. For the first time, I thought of what it might be like for an innocent man charged with a crime.

If he was lucky, he was not a pro football player with a glamorous blonde for a wife. The media ate up guys like that.

To illustrate: in the face of a dozen or more cameras, I was finally about to leave the jail and approached the last door that would free me. I turned the handle, but it wouldn't open. I tried again, and again no. Flash bulbs were popping and I was thinking, "Hell, I can't even get out of here, I can't open the damn door!" The man at the desk who pushed the buzzer for the electronic lock was talking to a reporter and was slow with his release. I called to him; it was almost a crazy kind of joke that I found somewhat amusing, so when we finally synchronized, I was at the tail end of a tired, wry smile.

This second of my life became an AP photograph that appeared all over the country. Someone would tell me later that it made me look like a sick pervert. Naturally, out of over twenty-five shots, they chose that one.

But I tried to keep things in perspective. I remembered how much good publicity I had received, some of which was better than I deserved. I was paying the price of being in the limelight, and feeling sorry for myself was not going to help.

I went back to my apartment. It was comforting to be home again, where I felt in control of myself. The supportive calls were still coming in and I was somewhat rejuvenated by them. But it was a tough night to get through. When you watch your life deteriorate on a TV screen, it really hurts. You are suddenly in the center of a nationwide scandal and there is nothing you can do about it.

At 11:30 Tom Landry called. He was very sympathetic but full of doubts about the consequences if I continued to play. He asked me to think about it from all points of view. How would the public react to my remaining with the team? Would the criticism of me increase, and if so, would that affect my performance? Would criticism be directed toward the team, and would it affect their playing?

I thought about it a minute and realized that he was making some valid points. I had to stay away until the case was legally resolved, or I would cause a great deal of abuse to be focused on the team, as well as myself. And this would certainly hamper the Cowboys' comeback.

There was no getting around it. I couldn't play.

The next morning I went out to the Cowboy training quarters, about six or seven miles northeast of town, through a pleasant area that's just beginning to be developed. The building itself was temporary, walled by corrugated metal but very pleasant inside, with thick carpets, a pleasant lounge, and inside the locker rooms huge individual compartments. It was all decorated in Cowboy blue, even the meeting rooms where strategy was discussed and films were shown, rooms with sliding panels to create smaller rooms for individual groupings—receivers, defensive secondary, running backs, and so on. It was simple and pleasant and perfect for its purpose. It had been a second home for me in the way an office can be for a man who loves his work.

So now I was leaving this home for what, at the moment, read as a two-week vacation. I maintained the belief that I would be back, so I talked to them again, I told them that I was going on the move list, the best solution for the time being, and I thanked them all for their support: it meant a lot to me.

After hearing what I had to say, they asked me to leave the meeting. They wanted to discuss it among themselves, hoping that maybe they could figure out some way in which I could play. So I went back to the locker room and sat by my compartment, all alone. The room was totally silent, and it crossed my mind that this was the first time I'd ever been in it without dozens of others, that its silence was ominous, suggestive of my changing status. I sat there, hands clasped in front of me, and I looked up at the rows of locker stalls, reading the names above them and suddenly feeling like a hero-worshiping fan who had somehow managed to sneak inside. Morton, Hayes, Lilly, Garrison . . . I was so locked into being a part of them. Green, Hill, Reeves, Renfro, Rentzel. Yes, Rentzel. This was me, this was what I did. I played on this team and these were my friends. I sweated with them, worked with them, won with them, suffered with them. I would be nothing without being a part of this team. Football had been the opening door to everything that was worthwhile

28

in my life (even Joey, I could not help thinking). And now all I could do was wonder if I'd ever be back.

My head was swimming with these things when Cornell Green beckoned me to come back to the meeting room. Lee Roy Jordan delivered the team message: yes, they all wanted me to play, they wanted very much for me to play, especially since they were winning ball games again and there was a chance that they could come through for the division title. But then, they understood the problem, that it was a bad situation for everyone; if I felt it was best that I go on the move list, they accepted it as an unfortunate reality. They appreciated my feelings and my concern for them. They wanted me to know that anything they could do for me, they would do it at the asking.

I was very touched. Lee Roy told it very well.

"You all will never know how much your support means to me," I said. "I promise you one thing, and remember this: no matter how bad things get, I won't ever quit. Ever. It may take a while, but I'll be back. So long."

And that was it. I walked out, unaware that I would never return.

"Say, did you hear that Lance Rentzel's problems have been solved?" Henny Youngman began telling his audiences. "Sure, he's just been traded to the Montreal Expos."

"There's no doubt about it anymore," said singer Don Cherry at a nightclub in Oklahoma City. "Lance Rentzel can really handle the fly pattern." My older brother, Del, was in the audience with his wife, Kay, and some business associates.

At a dinner show in Las Vegas: "If Rentzel ever plays for the Cowboys again, it'll only be during the exhibition season."

And so on.

29

I was dying in Dallas. There was nothing left for me there. By Wednesday all my thoughts were turned toward leaving town. I had to get away from the stares of everyone I met, everywhere I went. I didn't want to talk on the phone anymore, even to friendly callers; I didn't want to face my parents for the shame I had caused them. I woke up from bad dreams to face only sadness. The only pleasant hour in my day was when I talked to Joey.

I had worried about her, worried that there would be trouble for her because of me, that people in the audience would lay bad things on her, that the press would make a thing of it, calling more attention to the problem. She assured me that it was all going fine, that there was hardly any mention of it. Yes, she was fine. Yes, she loved me. Yes, she couldn't wait to be together with me again.

We decided to meet at our apartment in Los Angeles. She would finish her engagement on Wednesday night and fly to Los Angeles on Thursday morning. I would leave from Dallas at the same time. It was something I looked forward to, making the days seem bearable. I thought I could stand just about anything, knowing I was going to be with her again.

When I called her again on Wednesday night, however, something was different. I felt it in her tone. It was there, some negative thought, some intruding doubt. I didn't know what she was thinking and, foolishly, I didn't ask. I was too confused to ask, too worried to get beyond the need to be with her. "Lance," she said, "I've got to talk to you, I've really got to talk to you."

I said, OK, I'd see her tomorrow.

She said, "Yes," then paused, playing with her thoughts. "Could we go to Palm Springs, maybe that will be nice. . . ."

I said, "Sure, let's go to Palm Springs. We'll have a good time and forget about all the trouble. I need to do that. I'm afraid everything is going to collapse in on me."

"Lance . . ." She tried again. "Look, maybe we shouldn't go there."

"Joey, you just said you wanted to go."

"I know, but I want to *talk* to you."

"We'll talk. We'll talk. But let's have a good time, too. I need to get away from this for a while. We need a good time together. . . ."

Mother: We all have too much to remember. The next-door neighbor who pretends such compassion and immediately reports her version of the conversation to the Adamses. The traffic jam in front of our house on weekends—cars two abreast and bumper to bumper—gaping at our house as though it were the spot where Kennedy was assassinated. The people who throw on their brakes and sit gawking at me as though I had two heads when I go out in the afternoon to get the paper. The frightening phone calls from kooks and homosexuals. The Chicago Gay Alliance. "Don't you dare call this number again. My son is not one of you!" Both phones ringing the moment they're hung up. Men who called themselves "psychiatrists" saying they could cure Lance's problem. "My son has no problem!" The people who stop their cars and walk up on our lawn and take pictures of our house when I'm in full view working in the garden. The people who come in the night and take our beautiful Venetian stone dogs, which were cemented to their pedestals— presumably as souvenirs. The woman who calls the police at midnight impersonating me and reporting someone breaking in our garage, so that the police will descend on us from all directions in the middle of the night. The man who calls every Thursday morning between 3:45 and 4 A.M. and breathes into the phone, saying nothing for three or four calls, but on the last one sings an obscene song. . . .

I left Dallas Thursday morning. The smoggy L.A. basin, so ugly from the air, was like a beautiful red carpet to me. I taxied hurriedly to our apartment and exploded through the front door.

Joey . . . Joey?

There was no sign of her. I thought, well, maybe she was with Sid Gittler, our lawyer and business manager, and I called him. He didn't know where she was. Perhaps she'd gone out and would be back in a while, so I waited. I called up some of our friends, but they didn't know either. I called others. No one knew. I called Caesar's Palace, and they told me what I knew, that she'd checked out early in the morning. I felt a sick fear growing inside of me. I was thinking that she had come and gone to New York, or maybe Miami, but I couldn't really believe that, I didn't want to believe that, she wouldn't do that to me, not after what we'd planned.

Hours went by, wasted hours, hours that began to chew away at me. I hated this feeling of helplessness, I was too vulnerable, I didn't like what was happening to me at all. I had to do something. I called her number in New York, knowing that even if she was there, she wouldn't answer. If she was gone, she definitely wouldn't answer. She couldn't be gone. I couldn't believe anything except that she was going to come back. She had to come back. I tried to remember when something like this had happened before, when she didn't show up until later, when I was afraid like this, but it ended happily.

I told myself not to worry, I was making too big a thing out of this. I left a note for her and went out for something to eat, but I wasn't gone for an hour before I had to go back—I wanted to be there in case she returned, in case she called.

She did neither. Not on Thursday, not on Friday.

By then I was numb. The apartment was a prison. If I were a drinking man I'd have been drunk. I just sat there, stunned.

Finally I began to think again. This whole disastrous business had caught up with Joey. She had wanted to talk to me. She said it over and over: "Lance, I want to talk to you." All I could say was let's have a good time, forget about everything and have a good time. Joey didn't want that. She wanted to talk. She wanted what any sensible, troubled wife would want—to work out this difficult problem with her husband. I'd been a fool. I had driven her away; I just couldn't get myself to discuss it with her; I didn't realize that what I had done must have caused *her* anguish. I didn't let myself see that, because I really couldn't face the psychological meaning of my predicament. I was concentrating on my desperate situation, my bad luck, the bad publicity, and the struggle to get Paul Adams not to press charges and having to leave my beloved team.

We'd just go to Palm Springs and have a good time. Sure, a party. A long, fun-filled weekend party.

My God, what was the matter with me! What was *really* the matter with me!

I was all worn out with the emotion of this unbelievable two weeks, of being weary and sick at heart. I felt myself sinking into quicksand. I fell on the sofa and immediately got up. I had a fear of sitting there, afraid that sitting anywhere would force me to think, that I'd better do something, any sort of movement, any sort of activity, that if I sat down, I'd lie down, and if so, I'd somehow lose

33

control of my thoughts, I really didn't want to think about anything, I was afraid to think, because I knew what would come rushing through my head . . .

That I'd lost everything.

Everything I had.

Everything I'd worked for.

Everything I wanted.

There was nothing left now, nothing.

I had ruined my reputation and my career.

I had destroyed my marriage and driven away the only woman I'd ever really loved.

I paced the floor to keep from thinking, but the thoughts kept crowding in. My head spun with the realization that it was true, that as horrible as it sounded, it was absolutely true, that I was not overstating a thing, not a thing, that there really was nothing left, that I'd blown it all.

I wandered around my apartment the way that self-pitying list of failures was wandering around in my head. I walked from room to room, trying to cut off the flow of my rising panic: keep walking, keep walking as though somehow that would save me—from what? From myself? I didn't know, but I had to keep walking.

It was crazy. I felt crazy. Everything was lumped in my chest. Suddenly I heard a car—or I thought I heard a car—it was spinning rubber as it turned up the wet road a block or two away. Joey. I went out to the terrace to see, but I couldn't see for the curvature of the hillside and the height of the palm trees. I waited, ten seconds, twenty, thirty, long past the time when I would have seen a car coming into the driveway if it were her car. No, it wasn't Joey, it wouldn't be Joey, she was not coming back. Couldn't I see that? Couldn't I get that through my head?

I stood out there, no longer walking. There really was no room to walk on the terrace, three steps this way, two steps that way, there was only a rail and a view, high above the hills of the Sunset Strip. I thought, Go back inside and walk, you'd better move off here, this is no place for you to stand, not now, not the way you are now. But I stood frozen. I couldn't move. I looked out at the distant trees and houses and the lights coming on, and they started to blur together. Then I looked down, and everything below began to wobble. I was caught by panic now, I could feel it getting completely out of control. I was no longer myself, I was somebody else gripping the rail with an overwhelming urge to hurl himself down into that mass of trees and rocks, to smash the offending body that had somehow betrayed the golden image of Lance Rentzel, the winner, the guy who had everything.

II

I was twenty-seven years old with an uneven history—many high moments, and a few fairly low ones—but there was no doubt about the depth of this one: I definitely had hit rock bottom.

I was fully aware that this was no accidental set of coincidences. I was down because of forces within me that pulled me into it.

I wasn't in any position to ponder that question, not at the time. Deep down inside me, though, I knew there was something wrong with me, something very basic to the person I was. An Achilles' heel, with origins that went deep into my past and were as much a part of what I was as the dreams I dreamed, the way I drove a car, or a dozen other mysteries that could probably never really be explained.

Yet I had to try. I was unable to then, certainly not with any objectivity. Looking back on that dismal period, I wonder if there was ever anyone who was less equipped to truly examine himself than I was.

They say that linebackers are born so tough and mean, they come out biting the obstetrician's hand. I was born so fragile (five pounds, eight ounces), they put me in an incubator for twelve days.

Maybe that's the way receivers are born.

> *Mother: You started life as a tubular pregnancy and held onto a precarious landing in the uterus just the day before I went into the hospital for surgery. By all expert opinion, it was a miracle that you lived, and it always made me feel that God has a great purpose for your life. Life in any form is a miracle— yours, particularly so.*

My mother had a very difficult time carrying me, hemorrhaging frequently; she had to go to bed for weeks to save me. I was due on December 7, 1943, but arrived six weeks prematurely, on October 14.

It was probably the only time in my life I was early for anything.

Thomas Lance Rentzel, second son of Delos and Marjorie Rentzel. The heritage was primarily German, prosperous, and titled. My great-grandfather was Herr Wilhelm von Rentzel. Over a century ago, he raised fine horses for the German army and was an officer himself, in the cavalry. Part of the family came to Texas in 1875 and made a success in the carriage business. My father's mother died when he was a baby, and he grew up with four brothers and sisters without maternal care; he was shifted from one relative to another, denied the emotional security of a stable family upbringing.

My mother's grandfather, Peter Oster, was a Confederate drummer boy at Shiloh in the Civil War, and her family maintained a tremendous pride in their Southern heritage. She had an extremely proper background. My mother never heard her mother call her father anything but "Mr. Oster." Mr. Oster died leaving a young widow with three children, very little money, but a tremendous will to survive.

> *Mother: We had no luxuries and not all the necessities. My mother was so busy being father as well as mother, there was never any time to argue. When she said do something, we did it. . . . We loved her, and she loved us. She taught us to be grateful for what we had, a good family and good health, and that we could be anything we wanted to be with hard work and a good education. . . . She was proud and would not have accepted charity had it been available. . . . She believed that if we did the best we could, God would do the rest.*

My mom and dad met in Birmingham, Alabama. She was dating a man who shared an apartment with Del Rentzel, a radio operator for American Airlines. They met on a double date, and my dad impressed her so much, she came home and told her brother, "I just met the man I'm going to marry." On June 11, 1932, her prediction came true.

Apparently, I was an independent baby. I insisted on doing things my own way, wanting to feed myself as soon as possible. If I didn't like the food my mother served me, I'd turn the dish over on my head.

When I was about five, I remember getting upset once when Mom took me to a doctor for a penicillin shot without telling me. I hated shots, and I hated this one even worse because I was tricked into going. When she brought me home, I went up to my room and began packing.

"Where are you going?" she asked me.

"To find someone who won't fool me and take me to doctors who hurt."

"Well, you'd better call your father and say good-bye."

I did, and I told him why I was leaving.

"Well, good luck, son," my father said. "How much money do you have?"

"Fifty-eight cents. That should take care of me until I find someone who'll love me."

"Will you wait until I get home to say good-bye?"

I stood beside my suitcase until he arrived. He said he'd like to buy me a going-away present, so we went to a toy shop and he bought the biggest fire engine in the store. I decided that my parents loved me, so I stayed. I even went with my mother the next day and had another shot without saying a word.

Father: *He was a good boy, but he didn't like to be scolded. Once his mother corrected him and he called her "stupid." I suggested he apologize for that. He looked at me and repeated his opinion. So I whacked him, and he looked at me, cried a little bit, then said, "You're stupid." So I gave up—there wasn't much I could do about it. Then he went upstairs, pulled down his pants, and said, "Look what you did to my bottom, it's all red."*

Mother: *Your daddy had been pushed around as a child and was determined to give you the love he never had. He hated to discipline*

39

you for fear you all wouldn't love him. So I
had to assume much of the responsibilities. I
always resented the fact that when I told
you all to do something, your father would
often say, "I'll do it"; he never wanted you
to turn a hand around the house. This is the
only real bone of contention—except for the
fact that he traveled so much. . . .

My brother Del, Jr., was six years older than I. As a kid,
I didn't realize he had been very sick throughout his
childhood with severe allergy problems. I grew up very
much the opposite, very healthy, very well coordinated.
When I was a year and a half, I climbed out of my crib and
walked into my parents' room when everyone thought I
was asleep, and they all made a big fuss over me because I
had done this. If Del's difficulties frustrated them, my
prowess delighted them. I became the center of attention
in the family, the image of the ideal little kid would could
do everything, even tie my own shoelaces at the age of
two. I suppose it was true: I was blessed with all the things
that made parents proud.

Otherwise, Del and I were like most brothers. We fought
all the time. One Sunday morning when Dad took us to
church in Alexandria, Virginia, and he had to leave the
service for a while, Del found a cracked fishing bob under
the pew, pried it open, then clamped it shut on my ear.
The pain was so excruciating, I let out a furious yell and
lashed out at my brother in a rage. An usher rushed down
and dragged us outside as the whole congregation watched,
then held onto us until my father returned. For the first
time in my life, I was frightened of what my father might
do, especially when the usher told him what disgraceful
children we'd been. But my father became incensed at the
usher, not at us, telling him that he didn't need any advice

on how to raise his kids, that we were both good boys. I was greatly relieved. The usher caught hell instead of us. I couldn't have been happier.

> *Del, Jr.: I'd goad you into fights and you'd hit me as hard as you could and I'd laugh at you, infuriating you even more. You'd hammer away at my back or my arms, and I'd call you Sport. For some reason you used to hate it when I called you Sport. Anytime I wanted to make you mad, I'd say, "Hey, Sport." You were easygoing most of the time, but underneath, you really had a temper.*

When I was about eight or nine, I went to my mother and asked her for sixty dollars, I just had to have sixty dollars. She refused to give it to me, of course, certainly not unless I told her why, so finally I told her: I wanted to send away for the Charles Atlas body-building course so I could become strong enough to beat up Del.

I was six when my brother Chris was born, and before long I was picking on him the way Del picked on me. We went through years of daily turmoil, an endless battle among brothers who gave each other no peace but were fiercely united against outside attack.

My father began coaching me in sports when I was five. He had been a very good athlete himself, and I just fell right into it, especially since I was tremendously competitive. When I was in grade school, for example, there was an older boy who was always picking on my friends and me. I got so desperate to beat him that I challenged him to a fight every day. For weeks I'd come home badly bruised and cut up, but I finally won. After that, I had no further interest in him.

41

Father: *Lance was an exceptionally gifted boy. He could do everything. He learned to swim almost the first day he was in the water. He could handle a baseball bat with amazing power for a seven-year-old. He could throw and kick a football real well even in grade school. He was always extremely fast and could jump like a deer. His music teacher reported that he could go far with the piano, that he had excellent capacity to read music. He studied well and always got good grades in school.*

My parents have continually told us that we had a happy childhood, and I believe that by the usual criteria we did. There is no question but that Mom and Dad loved us, and for all the fighting among the three siblings, we did love each other.

Mother: *You and Chris and Del were alike in many ways, and so different in others. If Del and Chris got even a scratch, they'd let out a loud wail and come flying to show me, asking for me to "fix it." You never cried when you were hurt, only if you were enraged about something. Del and Chris were affectionate children from the time they were born—you never were. They liked to kiss and be kissed—you never did. I'd tell Del to run upstairs and get me something; he'd say, "Sure, Mother," but never move. You'd never answer, but you'd get it for me. I knew what you were thinking . . . it got so you would hardly tell me anything.*

My father was away much of the time, leading a busy life. He became undersecretary of Commerce for Transportation in President Harry Truman's administration; once he took me to the White House to meet him. The President gave me a penknife with an inscription on it: "Stolen from the Desk of Harry S Truman." Dad asked me to be careful, not to open it, but I characteristically disobeyed and ended up cutting myself, leaving a trail of blood on the White House rug.

My dad was a very prominent man in the world of avaiation; he even became friends with Howard Hughes. Sometimes our phone would ring in the middle of the night and Hughes would ask him to meet to discuss some new aviation project he had in mind. A limousine would come to our house, pick up Dad, and take him to a parking area from which a helicopter would then fly to an isolated airfield. There Hughes would be waiting in a B-29 in which he'd been living for days. In fact, he thought so much of Dad that he eventually asked him to be president of TWA, but my dad turned it down, and that cooled their friendship.

My father left the government in 1952 with the change of administration, to go to work with W. R. Grace & Company. We moved to Long Island, but we didn't see very much of him. He spent most of his time in South America, and I spent most of my time on the playgrounds. In fact, I developed my first case of hero-worship, a high school football player at Manhasset, where we lived. He was a running back named Jim Brown.

A year later, Dad was offered a new job in Oklahoma City and we moved again. I was old enough to be sorry to leave my friends, but I found it easy to make new ones. I went to the Nichols Hills School and attended through sixth grade, where I made straight A's. What I remembered most, however, was my dad speaking at my elementary school graduation exercises. He was a handsome guy with tremendous charm and wit, and the audience loved him. That night I felt very proud to be his son.

I had other noble aspirations, most of them designed to please my parents. My adolescence was geared to an emulation of their values. For example, I was religious. I believed in God. My folks took me to church and Sunday school. It was a part of our upbringing, and at the time I never questioned any aspect of it.

Meanwhile, just as my grandmother ran her household after the death of my grandfather, so my mom ran ours during the long absences of my dad.

> *Mother:* *You were six years old when our house caught fire, and you and Del had locked your bedroom door. Your uncle and I were frantically trying to break it down when you finally awoke. I grabbed you up and ran downstairs and put you outside and came back for Del, but the curtains on the landing caught fire, and Del bolted and ran back upstairs. The whole staircase was ablaze, and we pleaded outside for Del to jump. Not until the flames were inside his room did he attempt it. I caught him; he was almost twelve years old and if he'd jumped off a chair he'd have broken my back, but God propped me up and gave me strength this time, and he didn't touch the ground until I stood him up.*
>
> *Weeks later, in my sleep, I was crying out, "Help me save my baby!" Your daddy woke up and found me trying to unhook the screen, with you in my arms. I was going to*

throw you out of a three-story window with nothing but pavement below. He awakened me and calmed me down. There was no fire, but our apartment backed up to Sam Rayburn's apartment; he had built a fire in his fireplace, and the smoke had somehow backed into our apartment. In my sleep I had smelled the smoke. . . . Your daddy didn't go away for a long time—he was afraid to leave me.

Mother is a strong-willed woman, very devoted to us, and she impressed two things on us at all times: courtesy and neatness. We were taught to say, "Yes, ma'am," and to keep our rooms in perfect order. She even picked out all our clothes. (Whenever I didn't like what she bought, I would secretly give it to our maid, Viola, who was loved and respected as much as any member of the family.) She insisted that we really know the Bible, and kept on top of us to do our homework, practice piano, associate only with proper friends, come home at reasonable hours. She set very high standards, constantly challenging us to be the very best that it was possible to be. Everything we did, however small, every accomplishment we made, was praised to the skies.

When it became apparent that I really excelled in athletics, that I won prizes for my piano playing, that I got excellent grades in school, when I came to represent my parents' image of the ideal son—that, I suppose, is where the trouble began.

Retrospective dialogue (spring, 1972):

Del: *I was always very proud of my kid brother because when I was little, I was always very sick and never did well in sports. I didn't really miss it, though. I never was jealous of Lance or anything like that.*

Lance: *I admired the fact that Del and Chris never resented me. That's two great brothers. As for Mom and Dad, I think they were overly proud of me.*

Viola: *They were both proud of you. I think your father lived through you. He came to every game to watch.*

Del: *He never came to watch me drink beer at*
(lightly) *O.U. (Oklahoma University).*

Lance: *Maybe she put too much love on us because Dad was away so much.*

Viola: *She loved her house, but your mother's house was never really your home.*

Lance: *We could never go into the living room and sit on the fancy sofa.*

Viola: *No—you couldn't even rehearse your little band. Too much noise. Grease spots from the instruments and all. It would make her upset. Once Del wanted an old car and your mother wouldn't let him have it because she knew that he'd take it apart and she didn't want the driveway messed up. Of course, we were living right across from the Country Club. . . .*

Lance: *She used to force food on us. She used to serve brussels sprouts and Del and I, we couldn't stand them. It got so bad we used to put them in our pockets, so Mom would think we'd eaten them. Then she punished us because we messed up our pants.*

Viola: *You were always too sensitive about things.*

46

Now Del, he never got upset about it. His philosophy was that when he woke up in the morning, everything was going to be better.

Del: *I did my share of suffering. The worst time, though, was those two years at military school. I was sixteen, and everybody I knew was having a good time, and I'm learning how to kill people . . .*

Viola: *Del's interest was always in cars. For Lance, it was football and sports. And little Chris was interested in anything his big brothers did. The only time I ever saw you all agree on anything was when you didn't want to go to Europe.*

Del: *Isn't that terrible? The trip of a lifetime and we didn't want to go.*

Viola: *She was going to have the best-dressed kids in all of Europe. The things she bought you, luggage and all . . .*

Lance: *We were the three ugly Americans, all right. She couldn't understand why we hated that trip. . . .*

Del: *I think you have this thing, Lance; I mean, you get too emotional about her. Mom tries to baby me at times. Still does. It bothered me too when I was a kid, but the thing to do is ignore it. You should accept her the way she is. You can't change her. She's your mother. She loves you. That's the way she is. You can't spend your time worrying about being a momma's boy, it became an obsession with you.*

Lance: *Well, yeah . . . maybe.*

I didn't go to a public high school. Mother believed that the quality of education was less than inspiring. My older brother, Del, had been sent to military school because he had been too hard to discipline. The allegedly untroubled second son, me, was sent to Casady School, a small private institution with about 175 students and a high academic rating.

I took the entrance tests and registered the highest IQ in my group, and my family had enough money to be able to afford the tuition. The big question became, how good a school was it for a rebellious thirteen-year-old?

Even with hindsight, I am unable to judge its impact. There are fine things to remember about my years there, but how well did it prepare me for what became my future? If I had it to do all over again, if the choice were mine, would I go to Casady or one of the big public high schools in Oklahoma City?

I was mischievous and very, very wily. I developed a special talent for organizing mischief, then sitting back to watch others take the blame. My buddy in these ventures was a good friend named Bob Browne. We were amazingly skilled at setting up elaborate schemes to disrupt the classes, but others would always get blamed for them.

I spent so much time and energy stirring up trouble and avoiding punishment that I had no real inclination to learn anything. If I did get an education, it was purely by osmosis. My grades became barely passable; my concentration on studies was minimal. When I wasn't working out devious plots to create havoc, I was spending my time with girls.

I was interested in only the best-looking girls; appearances meant everything. Occasionally I would find myself hurt by a rejection. But I learned the best way to get over it: I'd get another one to take her place.

I was very reluctant to hurt anyone's feelings. I didn't have the capacity to say no to an invitation, even when I already had a date, because I didn't want to make someone dislike me. I would then find myself in fantastically complicated situations in which I'd make up all sorts of explanations to work my way out without hurting anyone. Once I accidentally asked two different girls to the same dance. Naturally they found out they both had the same escort. Deservedly, I ended up with no date at all.

We would have parties on Friday or Saturday night, a dozen or more fourteen-year-olds, and we'd be kissing all night long. The parents would be out for the evening, and we would be watched by the maid. Every once in a while, one would tell the parents about it: "Oh, my God, you should have seen it, they were just breaking their backs, they were kissing so hard!" and then the kid would get the tar whopped out of him for conducting such a party.

Which meant that the next party was at someone else's house, and the action went on as before.

I never had any sexual involvement in those years. By modern standards, I could be called a late starter.

Meanwhile, I was making a start in athletics. I sat on the bench my freshman year in football, but near the end of the season, when we were winning 38-0, I was sent into the game. The first time I carried the ball, I took off around end from the fifteen-yard line, broke a tackle, made a good move on the safety, and ran it in for a touchdown. I felt like a king. I was dating a girl I liked and she was proud of me. I went home and told Mom and Dad all about it, emphasizing that it was going to get in the paper the next day. I thought about that frequently the rest of the night, remembering the way the reporter had asked someone about me on the sidelines.

Suddenly, there it was. Lance Rentzel's first press notice.

It read: ". . . And then Rincle scored from the fifteen. . . ."

R-i-n-c-l-e.

I was crushed.

During my sophomore year, my reign of terror ended and all that mischievousness caught up with me. Teachers began pooling their information and decided that Bob Browne and I were the real troublemakers. We started to get kicked out of class frequently. The principal began to punish us. We were made to plant shrubs around the school grounds, paint stripes in the parking lot, sweep sidewalks, and pick up cigarette butts. But apparently I wasn't ready for rehabilitation. They began to make moves to expel us, an uncommon action at a select private school like Casady.

It might have happened. I really don't know how close they came. I don't know what my parents would have done, for the shame would have crushed them. Was I following in the footsteps of my older brother, Del? Would I, too, end up at military school, where they crush the rebelliousness out of you?

My athletic ability saved me. Our coach, Hoot Gibson (no relation to the movie cowboy), sensed that I would be a winner for him and didn't want to lose me—or Bob Browne. He went to the faculty meeting with a promise that he would straighten us out. A last-ditch effort, as it were. If he couldn't do it, no one else could.

He began to punish us after practice with extra wind sprints, endless sit-ups, laps around the field, then more wind sprints, sit-ups, and laps. He was all over us, chewing us out for every little mistake, giving us almost no breathing room. The way he figured it, desperate problems called for desperate solutions, and he was going the whole way.

I hated it, hated every day of it. I really don't know why I stayed there. I nursed all kinds of ideas about defying him, about refusing to move at a command to run another lap, about not showing up for practice on some contrived excuse. I didn't do any of these things because, somehow, I respected Coach Gibson a lot. I began to feel that this was exactly what I needed, someone to take me by the neck and stop me and knock some sense into me.

Then, too, there was Mrs. Margaret Tuck, my English teacher. I was always afraid of her sharp wit and biting tongue. To deny my fear, I made an effort to disrupt her classes. Incredibly, she supported me before the faculty. She would talk to me after class, encouraging me to work, to read, to express myself. She became a big help to me, and gradually I began to apply myself properly. My behavior and my grades showed it. I rose to the top of my class.

Since the age of six, I'd been taking piano lessons, and though I stopped in my prep school years, I still liked music, especially rock and roll. I started a combo and developed a pretty fair singing style in the process. I was only fifteen years old, but we managed to get our first booking in a place called the Lakeside Lounge in Oklahoma City, where we each got $5 a night, big money to us. There was only one fly in the ointment: the boss had a girl friend. She wore makeup an inch and a half thick, but it couldn't cover her lack of talent. Unfortunately the boss thought she could sing. After she tried out a few tunes with me, he wanted to fire the rest of my group and make stars out of us. He even offered to double my salary and give me billing on the sign outside. (He would save $10 on the deal.) But I refused—we were a combo and we would stay a combo—and he finally agreed.

I arrived on our opening night with sunglasses on, like my idol, Ray Charles. The dim lights of the lounge made me almost as blind as he, and when I came on stage, I bumped into the piano. The audience immediately thought, "It's really too bad. A nice-looking boy like that." They all felt very sorry for me and I soon realized they thought I was blind. I played up the blind bit after that by having one of my musicians lead me on and off the stage. I'd bump into things on purpose, and pretty soon I was getting tips from the sympathetic patrons. I became the star of the show.

Then my parents came. I had tried to impress them by telling them about the big money I was making, and though they suspected it was a low-class place, they weren't ready to walk into what was a real dive—the kind of place where the men came from work in their Texaco uniforms, where the room smells of cheap cigars, cheap whiskey, and bathroom deodorants. I watched Mom come through the door and saw her cringe. Even Dad was shocked. They had never been in a place like this for any reason at all, until now, and for the worst reason imaginable: to see me perform.

The owner then made a big announcement about the great duo that would start the show: Miss No Talent and me. She came out, leading the fifteen-year-old blind pianist, then sat on the piano like Helen Morgan and began singing directly to me in that phony sexy voice of hers: "I want to make love to you."

My mom must have really loved that.

There was more. I had asked the boss to make my parents feel at home, so he sat down with them.

"This is a nice place you have," my mother offered—words that must have killed her.

"Yeah, it's OK," he agreed. "We ain't had a fight here since last Thursday. Just a few guys got cut up—nothing serious."

We ended the set, and one of my musicians led me out. That was my last night at the Lakeside Lounge.

Later on that summer, our parents decided to give us some culture. To me, culture was the Mummers Theatre in Oklahoma City, where local actors brought new meaning to the works of Shakespeare and Tennessee Williams. Mom and Dad believed we would find real culture in Europe. They should have known we weren't ready for Europe, and Europe wasn't ready for us. The three of us didn't want to go, not in the least. After all, hamburgers were supposed to be scarce in Europe. Also Del and I didn't want to leave our girl friends, and Chris, who had been picked on for all of his eight years, didn't want to leave with us.

But this meant little to them. So we went. Two months of what might well be one of the most disastrous family trips in transatlantic history. Our first stop was London, where a pompous British chauffeur named Cecil met us in a Rolls-Royce limousine. Cecil, it developed, grew to loathe us very quickly and in two days was ready to quit his job. We kept him hopping for us, the center of our interests being a hamburger place called Wimpy's. When we weren't eating, we were fighting, usually in the back seat of the car. Mom and Dad, who sat in the front, would have to roll up the glass partition to shut out the noise.

Early every morning, Dad would wake us by barking, "All right, you new men—hit the floor!" His drill-sergeant routine amused us at first, but after a few days it got to be a pain. We also got tired of all the regimented tours. They really enjoyed that part of the trip, but we preferred to wander around on our own.

At the end of our London stay, Cecil drove us to the ferry over the English Channel. As we boarded the boat, he smiled for the first time.

Paris, Cannes, Monte Carlo, Rome: it was all pretty much the same. Hot dogs on top of the Eiffel Tower, topless showgirls at the Lido, playing roulette at the casino, and picking on Chris when we weren't searching for hamburgers.

By the time we got to Rome, even Mom and Dad couldn't wait to get home. I think they needed a rest from us. We cut short our stay in Italy and boarded the first available plane to the States.

That was the best part of the trip.

My junior year was unspectacular. I was growing up (my body was, anyway), which is about all I can say for it. I was closing in on six feet, 175 pounds, and gaining more speed. I enjoyed playing ball, all kinds of ball, and, just as much, I enjoyed the Casady girls. I won a few, lost a few. I rejoiced, I suffered. What is high school to a teen-age boy but a troubled transitional period before college? I suspect now that I held myself in intellectual limbo during those last two years. I concentrated on the pleasures and avoided any serious confrontations with my mind. I contented myself with a continuation of what my parents would call "achievement." In short, I kept them proud of me.

What was specifically worthy of note? The following, perhaps, if only because it still stands out in memory as a comic highlight:

A football game against U. S. Grant, the number-one team in the state of Oklahoma, a public high school on the south side of town. We were undefeated that season, but

Grant was a huge school with a huge squad and, because of the tough competition the players were accustomed to, was heavily favored. To make matters worse for us, we were playing them at their field, the scene of frequent gang fights between opposing student bodies. The Grant students, including some of the rosy-cheeked all-American-girl types, were there to greet us.

"Private school pussies!" they blasted our arrival.

That was something new. Raucous, threatening, intimidating, with just enough venom in the tone to make you wonder. I quickly figured out that they weren't taking us too seriously.

It was worse when we went out on the field. "Pussies . . . pussies!" sang out several thousand voices.

A challenge to one's manhood?

We played a sensational first half. In the first quarter I passed for a touchdown, and later I ran sixty-five yards for another. We left the field at half time leading 14–0.

Cheers, this time. The Grant girls were willing to grant us anything, except their virtue, which was probably long gone. It was a supreme moment for Casady.

Our triumph was short-lived. They tore us apart in the second half, wearing down our tired little squad with a host of fresh reserves and far more power than we could cope with. They won, 32–14.

The crowd immediately turned on us again. "Pussies . . . private school pussies!" they jeered as we left the field.

As we boarded the bus, they even threw dirty panties at us.

It took me months to get over the disappointment of that defeat. It was an experience that taught me a lesson I was to learn many more times: it pays to be a winner.

Then there was that hundred-yard dash in the state meet. Big track meet, key event. In the lane next to me, the defending champion was getting set in his starting blocks. I seemed not to care. He wondered about that and looked up at me questioningly.

I smiled. "You know what I was just thinking? In my whole life, I've never lost a race."

Not so, but he had no way of knowing. According to the records, he was faster than I. I never really expected to beat him, but my remark clearly made him nervous, upsetting his breathing, his timing, his control of his body. At the same time it gave me confidence. I beat him by a step and a half.

The interesting factor was that I had never tried a stunt like that before. I didn't plan it. It just came into my head at the moment and I let it out.

Is that what it takes to be a winner?

My first affair was with a lady of my choice—an attractive girl from another school. Once we began (and it was the first time for us both), we made love frequently, wherever we could find the time and the privacy. Inevitably there were problems, like the time we were in the back room of my home and heard someone coming; we quickly gathered our clothes and rushed into the bathroom. We dressed hurriedly, frantically, silently, only to come out and see my mom holding up a forgotten pair of panties.

She took us into the kitchen and lectured us on the dangers of premarital sex, and we were both very embarrassed. Naturally, then, we never made love again . . . certainly not until a few days later, when we found a more secluded place.

I always worked during the summers on the theory that I would learn responsibility—or so it was taught me. I started out as low man on the supermarket totem pole: a sack boy at the check-out counter. I was so low that what I wanted most was to be a can stamper. I really thought I could be great stamping prices on cans, much better than the second-rate talent they had. But those guys were older than I. They had already learned responsibility, and I was new at it. So I stayed as sack boy. Once I had to carry three huge sacks in the rain for a lady on a blustering Oklahoma day that almost blew me off my feet. But I got the sacks to her car, and by God, she tipped me a whole nickel. She wasn't poor, either. Her husband owned a chain of department stores. She could have afforded to tip me a dime. But then, maybe she was helping to teach me responsibility.

I was soon promoted to the bottle room, a storage room in the back where I had to stack thousands of returned bottles. I devised a magnificent maze of stacked cases about ten feet high, in the center of which I would sit in hiding and read comic books. Anytime I heard someone coming, I would shuffle bottles around to make it sound as if I was hard at work. One afternoon, I was sitting quietly in the middle of my maze reading, and I looked up to see my boss staring down at me. He had penetrated the maze in his crepe-soled shoes. He didn't fire me though; he knew my dad.

The worst job I had was working for an engineering company, out in the field with a survey crew; near Okeene, Oklahoma, the rattlesnake center of the world. It's famous for that. Every year they have an all-out rattlesnake hunt. And I was in Okeene working up to my hips in thick grass where no man could see a rattlesnake even if he spent all his time looking. You could hear them, though, and sometimes almost feel them. There were four surveyors on that crew. I was the youngest. I was there because my father knew the boss and I was supposed to be a hotshot in math. Instead of a slide rule, however, I had a snake-bit kit and I had to be ready to use it: I would first slash the wound, then suck out the venom. I wasn't really looking forward to doing that. I spent that first week walking tiptoe around the Okeene grasslands, all ready to die. After a while, I resigned myself to whatever fate might bring. If I was going to get bit, I'd get bit. Luckily for me, I didn't.

I didn't like Okeene. The first day I was there, I went to get something to eat and all they had was fried rattlesnake meat. It was as big in Okeene as chili was in Albuquerque. So I ordered it. But by the time it arrived, my mind had turned my stomach against it. When I tasted it, I went hungry.

One day, out in the field, we were attacked by a swarm of bugs, millions of them. I was slapping away, going crazy with the thought of being eaten alive, and I staggered out of control and fell clumsily into a muddy creek. I decided then that I preferred a desk job and got myself shifted to working on blueprints in the company's civil engineering section. I didn't particularly enjoy that either, but I never complained. Whenever I got bored, I just thought of Okeene.

My senior year at Casady was my best one by far. As they like to say of winning teams, it all came together at last. Since my interests were primarily with football by then, it was on the gridiron that life was at its best. Casady had a great season, and so did I. We were a solid team by then, a bunch of guys who cared about each other, who cared about winning. The word that coaches like to use is "pride." We had pride. I felt its special quality for the first time in my life that year. It manifests itself in difficult situations when the breaks start falling away, when the odds are stacked against you.

Like the game we played against Del City, a top-rated

and far more experienced team with what seemed like an army of giant players. Immediately it looked as if we were going to be massacred again; they had torn us to pieces in a practice scrimmage a few months before. On the first series of plays, they took the ball eighty-five yards for a touchdown, averaging over eight yards a play. On our first series, we got nowhere and punted. And then they scored again. It seemed pitiful. It looked as if it was going to be a rout. Then we got the ball and that something special happened. I could feel it in that first huddle. We all knew that if we didn't do it now, we were through. We started to move. Slowly, carefully, just enough for a few first downs. Then we began to punish *them* physically. It was marvelous the way linemen would return to the huddle after a five-yard gain wanting to hit them again. Late in the first quarter, Dale Mitchell threw me a long pass for a touchdown. On the next series he called a draw play, and I cut through the center as though I'd been shot out of a cannon. It was a fantastic experience, like a movie scene—the bodies seemed to be sliding away from me in slow motion as I broke through the secondary, reversed field, and sprinted to the end zone. After that we could see them quit, one by one. Even their star halfback. They simply gave up, and we whipped them 28-12.

Then there was the game against Perry, whose players averaged 215 pounds, their smallest lineman heavier than our biggest. Coach Hoot Gibson, sensing our apprehension, said the appropriate words of encouragement: "And remember, you guys: they may be a lot bigger than we are, but we're slower."

Well, it seemed funny at the time and it broke the tension. We won 26-8.

When the season ended, I was chosen to the 1960 High School All-American Team, along with Dick Butkus and Tucker Frederickson. It was quite an honor, but I knew luck had played an important part in it. Mose Simms, the head of the organization that picked the team, lived in Oklahoma City. Maybe he was partial to athletes from that area. Also the two games he saw me play were both against weaker opponents, and I scored four touchdowns in each. Nevertheless, the selection meant a great deal to me. Anyway, at least they were spelling my name correctly in the newspapers now.

Lance Rentzel runs as if the sheriff is after him. . . . The 6′ 180 lb. halfback with his pass catching ability and his stop-and-go twist and turn running downfield . . . Rentzel can fight his way down the middle or turn either corner. His shiftiness and speed enable him to get behind defenders on passes. He runs the 100 in 9.7. He also kicks off and is the Casady punter.

I began getting scholarship offers from dozens of colleges: Harvard, Yale, Princeton. The three service academies. The Big Ten. The Big Eight. I spent months trying to decide where to go.

All this publicity created problems. It's tough enough for a kid to be a celebrity, but it can be even tougher when he comes from a prominent family. My dad was at the peak of his success, and though he wasn't a millionaire, I became known as a millionaire's son—which made me nobody's favorite, except maybe another millionaire's son's, and I'm not too sure about that.

The fact that I was never the shy, retiring type also didn't help. I enjoyed the whole marvelous thing that was happening to me. Although I made it a point never to brag, I couldn't help if it showed. The day I made All-American, I went to the Split T, a big hangout in Oklahoma City. As I was leaving to get into my parents' Cadillac, three big carloads of kids pulled up to the car. They had big sticks and they started pounding on the side of the car with a frightening viciousness. I was really scared. I started to move as quickly as I could, but they cornered me, forcing me to the side of the road. I got out, not knowing what else to do, and I recognized some of them; they were from Harding High and they all hated Casady and its private school image.

"What the hell are you guys trying to do?" I called out.

They got out and started coming at me, sticks and all. I jumped back in my car and started off, and sure enough, they took off after me, a real movie-type chase through the streets, high speeds, screeching tires, cornering on two wheels, the works. They scared me so much, I ended up driving the wrong way on a one-way street and almost got into a series of head-on crashes. But I finally got away from them and drove into someone's driveway with my lights off and stayed there for about thirty minutes, just to be sure they weren't still waiting for me.

I remembered one of the faces—a guy named Bob. I had fought him once, when I was in ninth grade. It was the first real fight I'd ever been in. I had taken his girl away from him and he wanted revenge. He kept trying to pick fights with me every time we ran across each other. He was bigger than I was, so I tried to stay clear of him, but I had to put him down verbally to save face. It wasn't hard to make him look bad.

Finally he saw me in a park one day and came running toward me, and I knew that the time had come for me to stand and fight. I couldn't avoid it any longer. I turned to a friend to give him my wallet, and from out of nowhere Bob hit me, so hard that he knocked me out of my senses. My friend took me to his house, and they patched up the deep cut in my lip. I was out of my head, but I went out to find him. When I did, I went at him like a maniac, hitting him from every direction at once. I beat him savagely until others pulled me off in alarm. I really didn't come to my senses and return to anything like normal until later, when I was going home. I couldn't even remember what had happened.

This episode made me a local hero. Everyone began calling to congratulate me, but I couldn't enjoy my triumph. I felt so bad I went to bed and stayed there the rest of the day. I was afraid of all that fury in me; I didn't know where it had come from.

Now, years later, there he was again, with a dozen of his friends, big stick in hand, pounding on the Caddy.

There was over $300 damage to the car from the beating. Was that the price of fame?

I made All-City in basketball, baseball, track—all of which seemed to make some people even more resentful. Just before the conference basketball tournament, students at Saint Mark's, our big rivals, hung me in effigy, took shots at my dummy, then burned it in the streets. When I heard about it, I felt like Mussolini.

When I graduated from Casady that June, I hated to leave. They were rewarding years, all things considered, and I'd made a good name for myself.

After months of vacillation I finally decided to attend Oklahoma University because of its great football coach, Bud Wilkinson, a hero to every boy in the state. He had come to our home to visit me, and that had really done the trick. Mom cried because she wanted me to go to Princeton, cherishing its high-toned social and scholastic image, which was so important to her. I was far more interested in what happened on the gridiron than the interplay of social clubs.

I was also eager to break away from those apron strings.

When you've been loved to a somewhat stifling point by your mother, you become very conscious of a growing need for freedom. Like the time in high school when I got knocked out on the basketball court. I was lying on the floor dead to the world; my mother came out of the grandstand seats, right down to the edge of the court. She was worried, and I can't blame her for that. But I heard about it later, over and over, with all the accompanying jokes about how Momma was going to sit on the bench in the future, and take my temperature at half time, and wipe my brow during time-outs. Routine teasing, yes, but I didn't like it. I didn't like the fact that there was a certain amount of truth to this image of me.

So now I wanted my independence, and when I prepared to leave, my mother began to cry. Just as I knew she would. Her baby boy was going away to college. The trouble was, I was left with a sense of guilt. I wanted my freedom, I had reached the age when I could take it, when I was *supposed* to take it, but I still felt guilty. I confess, I didn't know how to handle it.

Nor did all the other pressures make my life any simpler. I had spent the last six years being prodded with the need to excel, to live up to my potential, to achieve. This became my purpose. And when you're a high school kid, it all makes perfect sense. You're being praised for your talents, rewarded for your performances. You're made to see that there are basic differences in people: some have it, some don't. You become one of the special people. Everybody is pleased with you, especially your parents.

You're eighteen years old and very full of yourself, you're going places, they say. You have that potential for greatness. You're going to be a star. "You have received a gift of talent from God," my mother said. "Now you owe it to God to use it properly." You're just a kid and you're asked to deal with God himself.

63

It gets to be very heavy. What you are to everyone is an extra special thing, and it scares you. To protect yourself, you learn to do what you're told. You're trained to do just that. You do what your parents, teachers, coaches, community leaders tell you to do. It's Pavlovian. You do what they say, you practice and train and perform under pressure, and they reward you. They make that very clear. Lots of accolades, publicity, approval, love.

You're scared, yes, but the system is there to take care of you. The machinery created by all those responsible citizens starts pushing you up and up and up. You really don't have to be frightened. Just play along and everything will be taken care of. You learn that all you have to do is perform at what you're good at.

Besides, it's fun. It turns out to be a whole lot of fun, that's for sure.

III

The college years are supposed to be the best years of your life. The University of Oklahoma, 21,000 students . . . the way I played my opening cards, I soon had the feeling that all of them hated me.

I was terribly naïve. I just didn't know that the average college student doesn't appreciate a brand-new freshman hotshot All-American rich kid from a private school—especially when he arrives in a new car (graduation gift from Dad) loaded with everything he could take from his bedroom just because he wanted his room to look nice. How stupid can a guy get? I had even brought along some of those awards to tack on the wall!

I settled in, and all of a sudden there was a steady stream of visitors to look in on me, big varsity football players included; I thought they just wanted to introduce themselves. . . . The word had spread: man, you've got to see this to believe it!

This was day number one, mind you, and already I was famous. I even had a nickname: "Tommy Trophy."

When I went out to football practice that day, I could feel the hostility even before I got to the field. It made me feel so awkward that I swiftly made matters worse. Equipment was issued very haphazardly to freshmen. You lined up for shoes, for example. What size? the guy asked. Ten, I said, thinking, well, maybe it's ten and a half, depending on the make of shoe, etc., and if so, I'd change it. When the shoe did not fit, I was too embarrassed to change it, so I wore a pair of my own. A bad mistake: they were Pumas with a white stripe down the side. Everyone else's were solid black. So the reaction was: there's Tommy Trophy, who's too good to wear shoes like the rest of us.

That made it rough. Even the freshman coach, Bobby Cornell, added fuel to the fire. On one play he was supposed to throw a flare pass to me as I swung out of the backfield. He did, but not without pointing at me—which let the linebackers know—and then he lobbed the ball up in the air to give them time to get to me like three armed tanks. We weren't even tackling, I didn't have any pads on, but they hit me like Dick Butkus. I got up as quickly as I could, hurting outside and inside, and everybody was smiling, very funny, so I got up smiling. I knew one thing for sure: it was going to get a lot worse before it got any better.

When I got back to my room, someone had taken the stuff I brought to school and hid it. A day later, there was garbage in my bed. And so on.

At times I would lose my temper, but it was like raging at windmills. All I was doing was gratifying my enemies. With the help of my roommate, Dale Mitchell, who was

66

also from Casady and was on a baseball scholarship, I learned to cool it. I cooled it, but I didn't like it.

Football was pure drudgery. The Bud Wilkinson system was based on proficiency in fundamentals. You spend all your time taking a step with your right foot, pivot, throwing your left shoulder into the dummy, and so on, and so on. Over and over. Practice was a series of drills that were as much fun as boot camp in the Marines. We spent the first two months doing this, not playing any games at all, yet spending almost three hours a day out there. I wasn't accustomed to that sort of thing. I loved football, but I loved to *play* the game. I'd hardly even touched the ball. At times we'd scrimmage against the varsity. Or, more accurately, we'd be the varsity's cannon fodder. They'd use us to practice plays against, beat us down, run over us.

It was also becoming very clear that a lot of the freshmen were damn good football players. There was nothing in my experience that could match this sort of competition. It was one thing to be ridiculed and hazed—it was something else when you felt you were being outclassed.

During this time many freshmen were quitting football. The drudgery was simply too great and the prospects of playing too dim. In my case there was a united effort on the part of coaches, players, trainers, grounds keepers, water boys, and stray dogs to see to it that I quit too.

"Now don't get paranoid," Dale warned me.

"Well, you'd be paranoid too, if everyone was plotting against you," I said.

I don't know why, but I didn't quit. I guess I was trying to prove something.

Then, finally, the freshmen had their first game. I got in as a quarterback, no less, because the others had gotten hurt. I was told what to do and did it, no passing, just hand off to the set backs, and so on. But just before the half ended, I took the ball myself, swept wide, then cut back against the flow, running sixty-eight yards only to be stopped on the one-yard line as the gun went off.

When I came off the field, the coaches looked at me as if I'd thrown an interception.

I got in the game again in the third quarter, for one series of downs, and I threw a touchdown pass. I ended the game as leading rusher and leading passer, though I'd played for only seven minutes. The coaches were so impressed, they didn't put me in the second (and last) game at all!

It was my first experience with the problem of favoritism and its counterpart. When there is an abundance of players to choose from, a coach has a difficult time deciding whom to play. He tends to like some, dislike others, and these evaluations can result from a variety of reactions that have little or nothing to do with ability or drive or attitude. It may be nothing more than the way a prospect wears his hair, or talks, or the way he chooses to decorate his room. I always preferred to think that talent would eventually overcome a coach's prejudices. But this is obviously a naïve concept, for talent needs to develop and grow, it needs a chance to show itself, it needs encouragement. In defense of the freshmen coaches at O.U., they had a lot of men and just so much room on the squad. The coaches could have their favorites and their victories too, so who could complain? Lance Rentzel? Who in the hell cared about *him!*

My desire to fit into college life brought me into the fraternity scene. I joined Kappa Sigma and managed to make a few friends. One winter day, however, I found myself in a dramatic conflict of interest, a real crisis of identity: a snowball fight had begun outside the fraternity house, started by passing members of the football team, clearly directed at members of the Kappa Sig house. I was inside when the action began, and the guys said to me, come on, aren't you coming out to fight?

So there I was. Who am I? A fraternity man or a football player? I really had to make up my mind. I decided to go with the football players—which should have surprised no one. Curiously, it surprised both sides and satisfied neither. I guess I should have stayed inside.

My problems seemed to crystallize in the spring at a sudden attack of a strange sickness, just before the football training season was to begin. I was running a very high fever. Dale Mitchell called my mom and told her she'd better come to Norman and take me to a doctor, an action I thought necessary since Dale was too busy with his classes and baseball to drive me home himself. But he wasn't too busy to help me down to the car when she arrived. However, in any crisis involving her kids, Mom handled everything herself. Not only did she come up to the third floor of a men's dorm, an unheard-of action in itself, but she proceeded to clean up my room and make my bed. A classic illustration of high-class momism, just what I needed to enhance my reputation. Needless to say, it became a favorite story around the dorm for months afterward.

When I got home, the doctor said it was either the worst case of mononucleosis he'd ever seen, or leukemia. My gums were so tender, I couldn't eat a soft-boiled egg. My mom spent her time taking care of me and crying.

Mother: When I was growing up, except for malaria, we were all healthy, but if anyone really got sick, they died. Daddy, Mama, my brother. This haunted me.

69

The tests finally showed it was mono, and it kept me in bed for three weeks, during which I lost about fifteen pounds, and made me end up missing two weeks of conditioning drills. When I got back, I was not supposed to do anything strenuous. A temporary assistant coach who was running those drills knew that too. Like a fool, I went out there trying to prove myself. Other than the coach, no one knew I'd been that sick, though they probably saw how bad I looked. This coach thought he was "Blood and Guts" Patton. He was making us run hundred-yard sprints in rapid succession, without rest. Players were dropping out from exhaustion, but not Lance Rentzel, he'd been through too much intimidation, he didn't want anyone to think he needed special favors. The coach said nothing, and I ran right back into bed with fever.

When I finally started spring practice with the varsity, I was amazed that I'd been placed on the third team, which was as high as any freshman could be. There were eight teams in all, maybe a hundred men all told, and I couldn't help thinking that somebody had goofed, or they'd simply shuffled the cards, or some malevolent coach wanted to prop me up so he could knock me down again, or even that my mom and dad had called Coach Wilkinson and begged him to be nice to me.

The trouble was, I still wasn't a very good fundamentals player, the classic Oklahoma type, and sure enough, by June I ended up on the fifth team.

The real practice began the first day of August. This was 1962, just at the start of my sophomore year. Wilkinson had a regimen that made us think we were prisoners on Devil's Island. Wake-up was at 5 A.M., the trainers banging on doors with iron fists, just to be certain you got up. We'd practice for two hours and then have breakfast—the purpose being to avoid the hottest part of the day. We'd meet at midmorning for talks, films, instructions; after lunch, more meetings until afternoon practice, another two hours on the field. We were allowed two hours for ourselves before bedtime at 9:30.

The workouts were pure misery. No matter what time we worked, the temperatures hovered around ninety degrees, and in the afternoons they'd climb to a hundred. With over ninety ballplayers, the competition for every position was enormous, and it followed that the hitting was savage. One practice drill we had, halfbacks would line up in the slot right over the tackle, facing a murderous defensive tackle named Glen Condren, whom we called Moose. Every day Moose would rack up a halfback, and we'd go in to dinner and say, well, the Moose got another one. A guy I knew, Arthur Davis, tried to manipulate the Moose, but the Moose hit him and down he went. He got up very slowly, then walked off the field and never came back. I quickly saw that there was no way to finesse Condren, you had to hit him before he had a chance to hit you. I did this, generating a sort of do-or-die feeling to give me courage. I survived all right, but then maybe Moose was getting tired. (Condren became a regular defensive end for the New York Giants until he hurt his knee.)

The pressures were tremendous. The coaches barked like tough marine drill sergeants, never letting up. Players dropped like flies. Sometimes I would think that this sort of work was designed to accomplish just that: get rid of the softies. It was all so miserable that on one afternoon when the rains came and the word was passed around that practice was called off, there was such joy in the athletes' dorm that guys were literally screaming, dancing in the halls, hugging each other like those newsreels of the liberation of Paris.

Meanwhile I was getting nowhere. The only attention anyone paid to me was comments about my family's wealth or my mother's love or the decor of my room. The assistant coaches also contributed: every day I showed up, someone would say, "Are *you* still here?"

I stayed, but I wasn't enjoying it.

Then there was one day that will serve as one of the greatest illustrations of torture ever exhibited on the athletic field. Afternoon practice, the second of the day. Temperature, ninety-nine degrees. Humidity, 100 percent. (It had rained all night.) Full pads, scrimmage. And when your group was removed from scrimmage, you didn't rest, you were brought to an adjacent practice field for continued work. I could hardly breathe. My mouth felt as if it were padded with cotton. All I could think of was water. I saw two players lose every bit of salt in their bodies and cramp up into coils of agony. They were rushed to the hospital. I saw another go crazy. He'd been knocked out and had been revived with smelling salts, and when they stood him on his feet, he went for Coach Wilkinson and began cursing him, then actually attacked him with his fists. The practice went on and on as though none of this were taking place. The sweat clung to our uniforms until they could not have been more soaked if we had stood under a shower. I had no idea how the quarterback could even call signals. The coaches were relentless (but then, they were allowed water) and it seemed to us that they were rejoicing in the punishment they were meting out. It made no sense, it wasn't practice; no one was able to perform, no one had the strength to learn, no plays were being timed, no blocking techniques were being perfected.

When the final whistle blew, I sank to my knees unable to move. The field was covered with bodies that could not rise. When I finally got back to the locker, I could not get my uniform off; I simply didn't have the strength. It was amazing, really amazing. I had lost over fifteen pounds, and several of the linemen had lost close to twenty-five. I did not get back to my dorm until well after dark, too

72

feeble to eat; I just wanted to drink and to sleep and, hopefully, to die. Why was I doing this? I wasn't even playing! I was on the fifth team, which is almost like having to pay to get in to see the game. I pulled myself together by promising my body and my soul that I was going to quit. There was nothing to prove by staying except my unbelievable stubbornness. No reason I could think of would justify my going to practice on the following day.

To cement this resolution, I called home to tell my dad. With hindsight, I don't know what might have happened to my life if he had been home and had sympathetically supported this decision. My mother was somewhat upset by it, suggesting that perhaps it would be best if I waited until I could talk it over with him, that it was not the sort of thing to treat lightly.

I hung up depressed by this impasse. The way I had left it with her, I would go back to practice, but only as a holding action. I didn't want to, I wasn't going to work hard, I would just be going through the motions while I waited to hear from my father.

Which is exactly what I did the following day. My body was there, but not my spirit. I faked it. Any football player knows how to do that, even the best, the hardest workers. We all go half speed at times, hoping that we can get away without being too obvious about it. I didn't even care. Incredibly, no one noticed. Maybe the coaches didn't care about me either.

Then Coach Wilkinson must have become worried about all the guys who were leaving the squad. He held a special meeting and talked about how quitters didn't have any pride. In fact, he read a poem about how important it was to stay with something that others do not have the courage to pursue, how there's a triumph in not quitting, how the purpose in a man's life is strengthened in the process. It was very inspirational, and I found myself tremendously moved. I said to myself, he was right, I had to stay with this, especially since I had come this far, especially since by now fully 200,000,000 Americans believed I was a quitter. I wasn't going to let them think they were right, not even after half of the guys who'd been hounding me since I'd arrived had already quit!

I went out that afternoon with a resurgence of grim determination—and before five minutes were over, I came off the field with a broken hand. I relaxed. The cast on my hand was a perfect tranquilizer. I went to meetings and daydreamed of heroic conquests to follow.

By this time I'd gotten to know a magnificent madman named Joe Don Looney, a running back of incredible speed and power. Unfortunately he was a little unpredictable, and the coach did not hold him in equally high regard. He sat on the bench during our first game against Syracuse, during which both teams went up and down the field with nobody crossing the goal line, what they call a strong defensive game. There were two minutes left and we were down 3–0. I was sitting with Joe Don, and suddenly he got up and walked over to the coach.

"Put me in, Coach," he said. "I'll win it for you."

It was the kind of line they use in movies that kids see on Saturday afternoon; the coach either barks back, "Get out of my sight!" or he sends you in with a glorious whack on your rump.

Wilkinson looked at Joe Don and merely nodded.

"OK," he said.

Two plays later, Joe Don broke off tackle, cut back down to the center, broke a few tackles, then raced sixty-eight yards to the goal line to win the game, 7–3.

He was amazing all season. In a game against Kansas, his first as a starter, when he was running very poorly and couldn't gain a yard, he went up to the coach and said,

74

"Take me out, Coach, my legs don't feel so good," and Wilkinson took him out. Then, late in the game with us behind, 7–6, Joe Don went back to him and said, "Put me in, Coach, my legs feel fine." And on the first play he ran sixty-two yards for a touchdown. We won, 13–7.

We had another Terrible Turk, a really wild guy named John Flynn. There is no way to explain him exactly, except to say he was the prototype of nonconformity. He couldn't handle rules of any kind, whether they were being imposed on him by society or coaches. He didn't care about practice, he wouldn't break a sweat. But in the games he was a standout, both offensively and defensively.

Meanwhile, Lance Rentzel, doubtful boy hero with broken hand, began to mend, and mending, he wanted to play.

I was still with the fifth team, and that meant I didn't go on the road trips. It also meant that, for home games, I would get to the locker room hours before game time to get taped in hopes of playing—only to be told once by the trainer as the first three teams arrived, "Sorry, son, you're going to have to leave now: the TEAM is coming."

Now *that* made me feel just great. I mean, I was *really* glad I didn't quit.

The week after my cast came off completely, we were about to leave for the big game against Texas, rated number one in the nation. Coach Wilkinson thought up a play at the end of practice where Ronny Fletcher, another stalwart fifth-teamer, and I were to go in as halfbacks. The quarterback was supposed to pitch to Ronny, who starts a sweep while I take off downfield, then Ronny, who could really throw the ball, lets loose to me. Terrific. We tried it twice, and it didn't work either time.

In the locker room the coach told me that there was no room on the plane going down to Dallas. "But if you can get down there yourself, I'll suit you up."

In short, I wouldn't have to pay to get in the ball park. But that was better than the alternative.

I had a hell of a time trying to get to Dallas. The car my girl and I were riding in broke down about twenty miles north of the Texas border, and we ended up hitchhiking with our suitcases, trying to arrive in time for the pre-game parties that night. We didn't get there until after midnight, but not too late for some pretty good college fun. I found a place to lie down around four in the morning, then woke up around eight with a bad hangover. Not knowing what time I was supposed to be at the stadium, I arrived a good two hours before the team did. It didn't help how stupid I felt. I had nothing else to do, so I went to the state fair they hold every year at the Texas–O.U. game, and just to keep myself in shape for the afternoon, I ate a couple of hot dogs and some cotton candy, and went on some of the rides. When I arrived at the locker room, my legs felt like soggy rolled-up newspapers, and my head was nowhere. I was thinking, so what, at least I'll see the game.

It was a big one, all right. The Cotton Bowl with 75,000 people, and Lance Rentzel all suited up, warming up as though he were Oklahoma's all-time pride and joy, then taking his usual seat at the end of the bench. A great game, as it turned out; we were three-touchdown underdogs, but we stayed right in there. Joe Don Looney was having a good day, and toward the end of the second quarter we were losing by a mere 6–0. It was anybody's ball game and every play seemed crucial.

We got the ball in the closing minutes of the half, and suddenly Wilkinson was looking up and down the bench, calling for Ronny Fletcher and me. Two seconds later, I had my helmet on and was running out onto the field for my first college play.

Lance Rentzel, sophomore, eighteen years old, was

76

actually on the most celebrated playing field in the South-west with instructions to the quarterback to call his play.

I was really shocked. I couldn't believe this was happening. I was hung over, tired as hell, legs hurting, dizzy, and scared out of my mind. I lined up and saw the defensive back much deeper than normal. And I was supposed to run past him—an absolute impossibility. I thought quickly that the quarterback would call a time-out or an audible, anything to stop what had to be disaster. Or maybe Ronny would just run with the ball.

I listened for the signals. No change. The ball was snapped and I took off, turning on whatever speed I could generate, trying to get behind this guy who never even let me get near him. I ran about thirty yards or so and then I thought I'd better turn around and see what was happening, an instinctive reaction, I suppose. I stopped short, turned, and the ball hit me in the chest. It surprised me so much I almost dropped it. Ronny had made his move, didn't know what else to do with the ball, so he threw it. It was one of the greatest thirty-eight-yard turn-ins ever made. A perfectly executed fluke. (Had I run a couple of yards farther before turning, the ball would have hit me in the back of the head, and I would have looked like a fool. But luck was with me this time.) I got tackled on their thirty-two and the crowd noise was deafening.

We returned to the huddle and Wilkinson hadn't sent in another play and nobody knew what else to do, so I suggested we try the same play on the other side. Ronny could throw from either side, even though we'd never practiced it. The play was called.

I lined up opposite Jim Hudson (who later was with the New York Jets) and he played me closer than the other defender had. I got behind him, moving at top speed, and Ronny let loose again. I caught the ball at the goal line, for a touchdown. Two plays. Two receptions, eighty-five yards. Six points. Ronny and I came back to the bench and were mobbed by our teammates. The crowd noise was unbelievable.

I spent the second half resting on my laurels. In fact, I didn't get back on the field again except for a last-period fight, a big team skirmish with everybody throwing wild punches. I went running out to add to my day with a left hook on some unsuspecting Texan. I brought my fist back to take a swing at someone, and just as I cut loose, somebody pushed a teammate in front of me and I caught him right on the button, knocking him down. He couldn't figure it, he looked up and was mad as hell, he thought I'd hit him on purpose. It was weeks before I could convince him it was an accident.

We lost the game 9-6, but the big news to me was that Lance Rentzel was moved up to the third team. In fact, the coach got a new play ready for the next game. I was to go downfield, fake inside, then outside, then end up going deep down the middle, with Ronny throwing again. It was another close game, so Wilkinson sent us in, and immediately they expected the pass. I didn't care; I was going to run that route so perfectly, I'd fake them out of their shoes. The ball was snapped and I took off, moving like a deer. I outran the halfback lined up in front of me, then faked out the safety. I cut to the goalpost and there was nobody near me. I made my last turn with that wonderfully exhilarated sense of anticipation, knowing I'd beaten them all, all I had to do was catch the football and I had another six points.

What I didn't know was that there'd been a whistle. The play had been stopped. And since 40,000 people had seen the route I'd run—including the entire Kansas defense—there was no touchdown for me this time.

I scored again in the following game against Kansas

State, and since we were beating the hell out of Colorado the week after, I got a real chance to play. I was doing fine until I made a bad mistake: I was taking the ball on a sweep when I saw that the defense had broken through, so I reversed my field, only to get shut off there too. I ended up losing nineteen yards trying to find daylight. It was the kind of thing that Wilkinson hated; it didn't matter that I'd intercepted a pass and gone a long way for a touchdown, or that I was one of the leading rushers in the game. What mattered was that I'd made that mistake and his confidence in me was shattered. For the balance of the season, I was put on lower and lower teams, hardly ever seeing action. The team didn't seem to be terribly upset by my fall from grace; they went on to win the rest of their games and ended up at the Orange Bowl on New Year's Day.

Wilkinson was determined to beat Bear Bryant, the only coach he'd ever lost to in a bowl game. He believed that, to do this, we had to be whipped into shape again, and he put us through a steady schedule of grueling two-a-day sessions all during the Christmas and New Year's holiday season, in the vacationland atmosphere of Miami.

We all fell into bed exhausted, but John Flynn was incredible. There was no way to stop him. He would sneak out for his nightly rounds and sneak back in just in time to go to practice. On the night before the game itself, the coach assigned to watch over him begged him to get a good night's sleep. But not Flynn. He laughed, lit up a cigarette, fixed himself a drink, and left the hotel for the rest of the evening.

In the locker room before the game, I watched him dress with a feeling of awe. I expected him to fall over and die. Then came an unexpected moment of drama: a group of secret service men filed into the locker room, followed by John F. Kennedy himself. The President was wishing us luck in that quiet, poised, friendly style of his while, in the adjoining bathroom, the ferocious sounds of Flynn's regular pre-game retching supplied a grotesque background to this moment

Flynn missed the President, but he didn't miss the game. He caught six passes on offense and made ten unassisted tackles, even though we lost 17–0.

I was proud to play on the same team as a man like that.

Then came "O" club initiation, for all the men who had lettered in a varsity sport, a terrifying ritual at Oklahoma that defied imagination. It was a day that I had dreaded more than any day of my life up to then.

It began at 5 A.M. when we each put on a burlap sack—our clothing for the entire day, including classes. A string was tied to the dick that ran up the body and over the outside of the sack. Attached to the string was a pencil that dangled in front of a cardboard sign on one's chest. We were obligated to get female signatures, the girls taking that pencil to sign the cardboard, knowing what happened when they pulled on it—very embarrassing and sometimes painful, depending on the puller.

After the lettermen checked all of the initiates to see that they were "dressed" correctly, we lined up in military formation and marched to all of the girls' dorms and sorority houses. Each of us was forced to sing romantic songs or recite nasty lyrics to the girl of our choice, and if the upperclassmen didn't like our performance, they shocked the hell out of us with "hot shots," battery-powered cattle prods that were used to move animals. They moved humans even better. No one ever got through this day without the torture of being shocked by those things. At the Student Union, some of us were forced to stand up on tables and sing more songs; others were lined up outside the women's dorms and forced to walk along a pole that crossed a small lake, only to be shocked if we fell off, and pushed off if we didn't.

But the climax of the terror was in the afternoon. At 5 P.M. we lined up in five rows outside the stadium for the finale. This began by our getting limburger cheese stuffed up our noses and garlic bulbs shoved into our mouths. Then they stripped us down to our jockstraps and painted us completely with red paint, topped off with a big white O on our chests. They poured glue, the kind that hardens in minutes, into our hair and under our armpits. They sat us down before a dish full of urine and garbage with orders to eat it. And we ate it, just to avoid that hot shot. They were always threatening us with those shocks, painful shocks on the nipple, the bottom of our feet, the ear—so we did what they told us to do, and we did it immediately. We swallowed anything, Lydia Pinkham menstrual fluid, shaving cream, anything. They poured wintergreen on our balls and made us rub it in, and it burned like hell.

Then they put sacks on our heads, completely blinding us, which was the worst thing of all. They came at us from all sides with the hot shots, driving us crazy because we couldn't see anything. At this point many guys cracked, they couldn't handle it. They just started running wild, running into walls, running into the goalposts—or the hot shot. A friend of mine named Steve Davis had gotten mad at one of the "O" club members and took a swing at him; it was a fatal mistake. They shocked him so many times he passed out, so they carried him off like a dead tiger on a pole. One guy was known to have a deathly fear of spiders, so they tied a tarantula on a string and let it run over his body while he lay there in horror, and when they took the sack off so he could see the thing, he almost had a heart attack. By the time they got that sack on me, I was petrified. I had to wear it for only ten minutes, but it seemed like at least two hours. I grabbed hold of a guy next to me and never let go. We just stood there in the dark, whimpering, waiting to be shocked. They shocked us a couple of times, then they hollered "Run!" and we ran with no idea where we were going.

This was followed by the grape race: they stuck grapes up our asses and made us crawl backward on all fours for fifty yards, and the guy who finished last had to eat everyone else's grapes. Anyone who dropped his grape got the hot shot for a reward. Next they dumped us into a huge tub of ice water—the sort they ice down Cokes in—and forced us to sink down in up to our necks. They had hot shots about three inches over the water line, just to be sure we stayed in. The cold felt good at first, but they kept us in for three minutes and it became unbearable. When they let me get out, I sprang out, my body screaming in pain.

Finally they led us to an assembly area, where they gave us the "O" Club oath. Without a doubt, the longest forty-five minutes of my life.

Lance Rentzel, varsity football letterman.

It was a preposterous initiation, barbaric, in a way, even though some of the coaches were there watching, just to see that it didn't get too sadistic. For me, it was the end of a year-long siege. I had come through when nobody expected me to. I had stayed with it and survived and won my letter. To some, that might sound like a silly thing, a hollow victory, a sign of false pride, whatever, but for me it was an achievement. I had defied all their abuse and ended up with their respect. I had done what a rich man's son from a prep school wasn't supposed to do. The world of college athletics was loaded with guys who were there on scholarships because they had no other way to get an education. Football was their only chance for a decent future. They ate all this crap because they *had* to. I didn't,

I didn't need the prospect of professional football to make a good life for myself. I had stuck it out because of pride and determination, and when they gave me that oath, there were guys who lined up to shake my hand who had never said a single civil word to me until that moment.

If I had it to do all over again, I'd have to say that this moment made it all worthwhile.

IV

Life progresses quickly when you're in college. When you're young you make tremendous changes, you take great strides, and before you know it, the year is over and something important has happened to you. I had spent 1961 and 1962 as everybody's patsy, a sort of punching bag for everybody's prejudices. But I had survived, and that was the key to it all. Having survived, I could go on to the next plateau.

Out of the cellar and into the parlor.

When I returned to play football for my junior year, there was little of the ridicule and derision I had become so accustomed to facing, but there was also little of the friendship I wanted. Curiously, the only two players who would open up to me were the two rebels, John Flynn and Joe Don Looney. They were really tremendous. They didn't give a damn about what others said or thought or pretended to think. They were completely themselves. They were very talented and tough. All I wanted to do was to get along, to be liked and respected, but the only guys with whom this was possible up to this point turned out to be these two eccentrics.

It could be said that, more than any other outside factor, they saved me from self-destruction. They indicated that I was no ordinary football player when everybody else refused to admit its possibility. They liked my looseness as a person. They never had any concern for images, not mine, not theirs, not anyone's. They didn't care if a guy was rich or poor or both, they looked for the independent spirit. They were sincere. Anything phony repulsed them. They liked me, and by God, I needed that.

So, when I started at halfback alongside of Joe Don in the backfield, with John at end, I had taken one of those sudden giant strides.

I would finish out the year, but Joe Don wouldn't. He just didn't have the patience to be a disciplined part of a team. If he didn't feel like it, he simply didn't work. Early in the season, before the Texas game, he was fooling around at practice and Coach Wilkinson said if he wasn't going to put out, he could just go on in. Joe Don looked at him and then called his bluff, I guess; he picked up his helmet and left. Wilkinson gestured for him to come back, that he'd forgotten about his being hurt. The other guys didn't appreciate the way Looney had defied the coach and gotten away with it. Wilkinson recognized this and kicked him off the squad a week later.

Despite that, Looney was potentially so great, he was a first-round draft pick by the New York Giants that winter, in the belief that he could be tamed. It never happened. He went through several teams, always a problem, and eventually dropped out of football.

85

It was pretty much the same with Flynn. After the season ended, he was suspended from school for failing to attend any of his classes. Although he could have been an outstanding pro, he wasn't particularly interested and went on to other things. Curiously enough, he ended up as an insurance salesman, the epitome of conformity.

I played a lot of football in my junior year. I began making friends on the club, like Ralph Neely, an All-American tackle, whose friendship grew steadily and has lasted for years. It was the sort of thing that did wonders for my state of mind. For the last two years, I had been going with Marcia Evarts, a lovely, intelligent, loyal, and understanding creature. She was studying physiotherapy and intended to make it a career, showing an ambition most beautiful girls do not have. They are content to float through college trying to pick out the most likely prospect for a husband, or to cultivate the surface qualities of an educated person. I liked women who wanted to be something in their own right, to contend with life on their own. I thought of myself as pretty much of a kid barely out of adolescence, but even then someone like Marcia made the best sense to me.

Still, I wasn't mature enough to handle it properly. We would argue a lot, and I know now it was mostly because of me. I needed and wanted her, but could not handle the responsibility of the relationship. I'd get angry at her, though I was really getting angry at myself. Once I threw an expensive book at her, sending it sailing over her head into a cluster of shrubs; so I had to go climbing among them to find it. After thirty minutes of searching, the book still could not be found—it was all so crazy, we suddenly broke out laughing. After another fight over a trivial matter, I returned all her pictures and gifts to her sorority, and she then returned my fraternity pin. That bothered me. I went to New Orleans for the weekend and got drunk. I couldn't stop thinking about it and finally called her at four in the morning, only to have her hang up on me.

She had more than enough reason to complain about me. For one thing, I was always late, which isn't good for a girl's ego. For another, I took too much for granted. Or, as a girl would put it, I didn't make her feel "special" as much as I should have. On one occasion I was determined to show Marcia how important she was to me. I decided to take her out to a big formal dance and do the whole evening in the best style. I put on a tux, bought her a fantastic orchid—then ran out of gas on the way to her dorm.

I thought, hell, now I'm going to be late, so I tried a short cut to the gas station by vaulting over a mesh wire fence, but my jacket was open and got caught, jarring me off balance. I fell to the ground and started rolling down a hillside. It was so steep, I couldn't stop myself from tumbling through maybe thirty or forty feet of brambles and shrubs, during which I really got scratched up, my clothes torn and muddy, a real mess. I got the gas, walked back to the car, somehow managing to spill some gas on my pants, drove back to fill the tank and return the gas can, drove to Marcia's dorm . . . late, of course.

I handed her the orchid, but all she could smell was gasoline.

I said, "You won't believe this, Marcia, but—"

She waved it off, not interested in any explanations. We went out and it wasn't mentioned again.

By and large, we got along very well. I always felt proud to be with her, to be seen with her, to know that she cared for me. I was much the better for the relationship. However, I rather doubt that it worked as well for her.

I cared a great deal for Marcia, but my energies were primarily directed into football. I was just beginning really to feel my potential, and I kept wanting more. I'd frequently run the previous game over and over in my head as though my mind were a stop-action, slow-motion, instant replay machine. I'd relive the good plays I'd made and try to learn from my mistakes. This sort of drive was new to me and not at all typical.

It was a good season for me, and I learned a lot more than I could possibly show. I felt like an old pro when we went back to Dallas and our annual game against Texas. There I was, the kid who had caught those two passes in a row and scored O.U.'s first and only touchdown, the kid who had hitchhiked to Dallas because he wasn't even part of the traveling squad, the kid who had never even been in a college game before. Dallas sportswriter Gary Cartwright even wrote a feature piece about me, a first in my college career. "Last year," he wrote, "they didn't even know his name in the press box." It wasn't until after I'd scored that they found out who I was. This year I was the starting halfback.

It turned out to be not much of a day for me or my team. We lost 28-7, and I made no great contribution, certainly nothing like the year before. Texas took our place as the number-one team in the country and finished the season as national champions.

I spent most of the next game, against Kansas, on the bench, having hurt my knee, and watched the greatest breakaway runner in the Big Eight, Gale Sayers, gain a hundred yards. Fortunately for us, he fumbled in the last period and we managed to beat them by three points.

On the following Saturday, I rushed for eighty-four yards in five carries and returned a punt seventy-one yards for a touchdown.

I was developing into what Bud Wilkinson would call a

good fundamental football player, not just big and fast and shifty, but disciplined and reliable. I was not about to lose nineteen yards on a single play through a stupid error in judgment. I was also not about to fumble very often. Fumbling is mostly the result of a lack of concentration, a drift into carelessness. Occasionally a player will get in a real hard shot on your arm and the ball comes popping out. But it's carelessness more than anything else. More games are won and lost because of fumbles than through any other single error (except perhaps interceptions).

I fumbled four times in one game that fall. It was the day after John F. Kennedy was assassinated. The truth was, I didn't want to play. We were up in Lincoln, Nebraska, for the Big Eight Conference Championship, just coming off practice on the day before the game, and we heard the news in the locker room. It knocked the spirit right out of me. The thought of this happening in America really frightened and depressed me. I had a special feeling for him as the type of man I admired, I liked what he stood for, he presented a good image to the world. Now he was dead, murdered, and I couldn't get it out of my head. A lot of the players were really upset; some cried openly and everybody was completely silent. We then heard that a lot of games around the country were being canceled, and I hoped that ours would be called off too. It wasn't, because it was necessary to determine who went to the Orange Bowl.

So I went out there that afternoon with only part of me working. I could not get myself properly geared to play. I tried. I talked to myself. I kept talking to the others. I hollered louder and more often than I ever did. And I fumbled, repeatedly.

We lost 29–20, largely because of my failure to concentrate. It bothered me for months because I felt I had cost our team the title.

Nebraska went to the Orange Bowl, and Oklahoma went home for the winter.

There was a certificate I received that summer: very fancy, with embossed lettering and a seal with red, white, and blue ribbons attached. It read: "This is to certify that THOMAS LANCE RENTZEL has been selected to appear in the 1964–65 edition of *Who's Who Among Students in American Universities and Colleges* from the University of Oklahoma. . . ."

That certificate (plus a dime) got you a ride on the local bus, but my mom thought I'd just won the Nobel Prize.

I spent most of the summer building up my body, following a regimen recommended by Joe Don Looney. I lifted weights, took steroids to add weight, and ran to keep up my speed. When I arrived for preseason training, I weighed 215 pounds, far more than I'd ever been, and I hadn't lost a step. Suddenly I was as big as any back on the squad.

I was ready for the season to begin. In the opener against Maryland, I caught a pass and ran ninety yards for a touchdown, winning the game in the closing minutes. It was the longest pass play in O.U. history. We lost again to Texas in our third game, but I think it was the best I ever played in college. It was quite an honor when I read that Tommy Nobis, a great linebacker, said after the game that I was the best back he had played against.

My senior year was far better than I expected, and almost as good as I had hoped. I quote from one article midway through the season: "When it comes to offensive versatility, Lance Rentzel of Oklahoma University and Gale Sayers of Kansas are at the top of the list. Sayers does everything but punt; Rentzel does everything."

The punting was something I'd walked into in college.

I'd kicked a lot in high school but stayed away from it in college. Ask any kicker and he'll tell you why: it's not good for your legs, especially the knees. If you're a running back, it creates problems, often leaving you with hamstring pulls, the nemesis of all runners. The only thing worse than being a punter is to be on the coverage team, racing downfield to tackle the guy who receives it. When our regular punter got hurt, I stepped in to replace him, even though I hadn't punted all season. That way I wouldn't have to cover any punts, which, in practice, amounted to wind sprints. It was one of those great instants when everything comes together: I kicked the ball almost the length of the field, farther than I'd ever done before.

From then on, I was our punter.

By this time, I believe I had earned the respect of my teammates and coaches. For example, I was having a bad time at practice one day, and an assistant got on my back about it. I walked off the field furious. If this had happened two years before, no one would have bothered to understand my side of it, and it would have been held against me completely. This time Jay O'Neal, the head offensive coach, put his hand on my shoulder and eased my anger: "Don't let it get you down, Lance. We have great respect for you. You've come a long way." A small story, no doubt; but to me, it meant everything.

The press kept the rich-man's-son fable alive. "The millionaire with a wealth of talent," they called me. Local reporters were not above laying it on a bit thickly: "Lance Rentzel, Oklahoma's fast, flaxen-haired halfback, majors in math, plinks rhythm-and-blues on the piano, and leads the O.U. Sooners in six departments. . . ."

Inevitably, my mom would get into the act, though it's hard to blame her for this particular scene. I thought I was relatively free of all those embarrassing references to her

91

until one day, in the locker room, a fellow named George Stokes related an incident at the previous game where his mother had sat not far from mine. Apparently, at one of my better moments, Mom had gotten all excited and cried out, "Isn't my baby wonderful!"

Innocuous enough, to be sure, though as soon as he told the story, I knew I was in for trouble. Sure enough, someone called me "Wonderbaby" in the shower the next day. And the day after, a rhythmic chant began during calisthenics as we went through bends and stretches: "One, two, wonderbaby—one, two, wonderbaby . . ." This time it was all in fun, but it went on for a couple of weeks, penetrating my fragile crust in a way that nothing else could. It got to the point that when my parents would come on the field after a game as I was walking off to the locker room, I would deliberately not see them—and if the confrontation was unavoidable, I'd walk away telling them I'd see them later. I just didn't want the players to see me in situations involving them. Although I was friends with everyone on the team now, I wanted to erase that rich kid—momma's boy image for good.

All in all, it was a great year, and we ended up with an invitation to play Florida State in the Gator Bowl in Jacksonville. In the Big Eight Conference statistics, I finished with a list of impressive numbers after my name: ninth in total offense; fifth in rushing, with an average of 5.5 yards per carry, the highest in the league; second in pass receiving; second in punting (average punt: 42.5 yards); sixth in punt returns; sixth in kickoff returns; fourth in total scoring. All Conference Halfback. Selected to the College All-Stars, the biggest honor of all for me.

All this was a rapidly evolving condition, coming out of only ten successive games—a state of triumph had been reached in ten short weeks. From relative obscurity on Labor Day to fame by Thanksgiving, and suddenly, there I was, a second-round draft choice of the Minnesota Vikings. Two months before, I was not even a name in their scouting reports. I had never thought of football as a career, primarily because I didn't believe I'd ever be good enough. After all those blows to my ego, I had no confidence in myself until I could prove it to everyone else.

I signed with the Vikings after one of those typically wild competitive weekends when rival teams and leagues came around to bid for my services. The Vikings even sent a "baby-sitter" down to keep me company—just to be sure I didn't make a better deal with Buffalo, an AFL club that was more than willing to try. My bonus was substantial enough, $21,000, but if I'd been smarter, no doubt I would have had a lawyer or business manager handle the negotiations. But I was naïve about financial matters, and I was more interested in getting the hassling over with as quickly as possible.

Three teammates of mine were also drafted by the pros. We were all advised by the club representatives that we could save a lot of money by signing in December, before the New Year, splitting the bonus and the salary over two years instead of paying taxes all in one. It made sense enough, and we did it. And it was a widespread practice among all college players who were about to turn professional.

But, as it turned out, I couldn't have made a bigger mistake.

The seniors on the team left for Jacksonville with vivid memories of our "vacation" in Miami two years before, but things were different this time. Our practices were much easier, and so our morale was significantly higher. I was looking forward to my last college game, and all that it represented. I wanted it to be a big one, and I primed myself for it. Then, the night before the game, the news broke that Ralph Neely had signed a contract with the

Houston Oilers, a clear violation of his amateur standing.

The coach called me up early the next morning. He asked if I had signed a contract too. I could have said no, I could have lied, and that would have been the end of it. But I told him I had. He said he'd talk to me at the team meeting an hour later. When I walked into the meeting room, I found out that all four of us had been kicked off the club, just like that, no hearing, no warning, we were simply asked to leave. It really hurt me to see the crushed looks on my teammates' faces as we walked out of the room.

I immediately packed and left, running into some of the guys in the elevator on the way down.

All I could say was, "I'm sorry."

All they could say was nothing.

I was extremely upset. Even my scholarship at O.U. was canceled. Nevertheless, I respected the way our coaching staff handled the matter. Ralph Neely was the only one they were forced to take action against, since only his signing had been made public. But the coaches were honest enough to get rid of everyone who had broken the rules, knowing that it would take the heart out of our team and practically ensure defeat.

Norm Van Brocklin, coach of the Vikings, was down to see the game, and I went over to his hotel room, so we could figure out our next move. He tried hard to make me feel better, but it didn't help much. I told him, to hell with it, I didn't care about playing pro ball anymore, and I tore up my Viking contract. I just ripped it up and gave him the pieces. He was sympathetic and eventually talked me out of quitting. He said he would have a new contract drawn up, including payment to replace my canceled scholarship.

I didn't want to stay in Jacksonville, so we decided to go to Miami. We arrived just in time to see, on TV, Florida State beat O.U. badly. It wasn't a pleasant experience at all, because it made me realize how much I had let the team down. "What a way to end a career," I kept saying to myself. I couldn't stop thinking of the players' faces as I left that meeting room the day before. So I went out and proceeded to get loaded. At one of the many clubs I visited that evening, I ran into a NFL scout I knew. He told me that five of Florida State's best players, all of whom had done very well that afternoon, had signed professional contracts before the game. I was a little bitter at first, but then I came to the conclusion that it was only fair that I should be punished because I got caught. Kicking out some of their players wasn't going to make me any less guilty.

The next day Van Brocklin and I went to New Orleans, for no better reason than that I wanted to go to New Orleans. I was so hung over and tired I could barely stand up. Stan West, one of Norm's assistant coaches, met us at the airport, and we all got into a cab to go to our hotel. The first thing the driver said was, "Did you hear about those bums who got kicked off the Oklahoma team?" and he held up the newspaper with big headlines and pictures smeared all over it—mine included.

For the entire ride, he talked of nothing else, and nothing he said about Van Brocklin or me had even the slightest trace of sympathy, which was understandable. "Sellout," he called me. "Unethical," he called Van Brocklin. It was funny, I suppose, and we fought back laughter until the end, when Norm apologized to the driver for not having enough money to pay, offering his credit card for security while he went inside to cash a check. When the cab driver saw the name, he almost fainted. We laughed so hard, I almost forgot how bad I felt.

I had a fine time there, leaving with a much lighter heart than when I'd come. I liked Van Brocklin; he was a lot of fun to be around. I looked forward to the start of my pro career with Minnesota, especially since Marcia, who was from the Minneapolis area, would be there.

When I got back to Oklahoma City, Mom was in the middle of the holiday social swirl. She wanted me to be an escort at the Debutante Ball. I didn't really want to go, but I obliged her and dressed up in my tuxedo.

Wonderbaby was home. . . .

The Senior Bowl, held in Mobile, Alabama, is a sort of final prize for some of the top college players after all the major bowl games have been played. Its promotion is based on that ageless rivalry of North vs. South, but nobody north of Charleston takes the trouble to attend. The players don't get fired up about the geographical rivalry. The winners get $500 more per man than the losers.

I accepted an invitation to play, although I wished I'd been invited to the Hula Bowl in Hawaii. As far as I was concerned, Mobile was not one of the South's great cities, and it certainly didn't compare to Honolulu.

For reasons that were too confusing for me to figure out, I was listed on the North team, but that's Oklahoma for you. After all, it *is* north of Texas, isn't it? That didn't bother me too much, but it didn't help me any when I found myself in a bit of trouble—as usual.

I was sitting in a nightclub in Mobile when I met a blonde from Germany who really turned me on. One thing led to another, and we were hitting it off beautifully when her ex-boyfriend showed up unexpectedly. A local lad, of course, and very Southern. He started to give her a bad time, and I could see that she was afraid of him: he had a weird, violent look. Chivalrous as always, I defended my new lady friend. "Why don't you leave her alone, buddy?" I said, now a Yankee.

He didn't like that. "Have you ever been in the army?" he asked challengingly.

"No."

"Have you ever been in the Special Forces?"

"Now, if I've never been in the army, how in the hell could I have been in the Special Forces?"

Everybody laughed at that, and he responded with a new wave of resentment, scowled a few times, then turned on his heels and left.

The fräulein was relieved and delighted, so much so that she wanted me to take her home for the night; she would feel more secure that way. "Well, all right—if you insist. . . ." All I had to do was be at the team breakfast by 7:15 A.M.

Everything went well until the Civil War began again, this time at 6 A.M. I heard someone walking in the apartment, and the next thing I see is that guy all dressed up in his paratroop uniform: boots, helmet, ribbons—and a big lead pipe in his hands.

There we were, in her bed, naked. As I looked at that pipe, I immediately tried to figure out if some diplomatic phraseology on my part could lead to a friendly discussion of this whole misunderstanding. No chance.

He went for the girl, pipe in one hand, her throat in the other.

"Hey," I hollered, "take your hands off her!"

Wham! The pipe crashed down on the pillow, just grazing my ear. I didn't know if he was trying to hit me or not, but if he was trying to scare me, he did a damn good job of it. I could see my parents picking up the paper and reading, "Nude football star found murdered." My mind was racing like mad. It was crazy, but all I could think of was that I was going to have to defend myself without a stitch on. It didn't seem quite fair. He had his clothes and the pipe too.

She was crying, terrified. I would have cried too—if there was a chance it would help me any. I wasn't above anything at this point. I thought I might as well go down swinging, so I decided on bravado.

"I'm not impressed," I said, mustering up my courage. "Only a chicken-shit would use a pipe. Just step back and let me get out of bed and I'll whip your ass, lead pipe or not!"

He glared at me for a second, then started coming at me. I thought, well, it was a nice try. . . .

Then, for some unknown reason, he turned and walked out of the place.

Saved!

I lay there sweating, my heart pounding furiously. She grabbed hold of me and pressed against me, wanting to repay me in her own special way. Any man who could make love at this point was unquestionably the world's greatest stud. At the moment, I was more interested in locking the door. For the next couple of hours I just stayed in bed, thinking about how good it was to be alive. I ended up missing breakfast, a meeting, and practice. But that had become the least of my worries.

That afternoon George Wilson, the head coach of the North team, asked where I'd been that morning.

"You wouldn't believe me if I told you," I replied.

What could he do? He walked away, muttering to himself.

But an hour later, the fräulein showed up, and all heads turned. We hadn't been getting the cream of Mobile's crop. After all, we were Yankees. So when she walked up to the edge of the field, practice sort of stopped. She wanted to know if I was OK, if I'd been hurt, if I would stay over at her place again that night in case our friend with the pipe dropped by for a return visit. On and on she went, until I saw George Wilson standing right behind me.

98

I did a lot of running that afternoon.

As for the game, I'd fooled around so much, I was certain I wouldn't play. So I sat on the bench, reading the program. Then one of our cornerbacks got hurt.

"Rentzel!"

Me, a cornerback? I never played cornerback.

"Get in there!" he barked.

There was nothing to do. On the first play, who should line up against me but a wide receiver named Bob Hayes. ("He's quick," the coach had warned me.) Figuring my best chance was to intimidate him, I knocked him on his ass the first play. He didn't like that at all. After that, I covered him like a dirty shirt on every play. I did everything but tie his shoelaces together. I wasn't going to let him do a damn thing.

We were beating them 7–0, but in the fourth quarter the quarterback threw Hayes a long pass and he went fifty-three yards to tie the game up, which was the way it ended. The quarterback's name was Namath.

As I said before, I never did like Mobile.

V

I graduated in June, 1965. I went through the commence-
ment ritual with strong emotions; these had been four
dramatic years. I had started out on the bottom but slowly
made my way up to the top of the college totem pole. It
was really a terrible-wonderful experience.

There is no way that a twenty-one-year-old can understand the impact. You're in a country where a twenty-
one-year-old could not possibly attract more attention
(except as a movie star or a rock musician). You've been
pressured since you first showed potential talent, molded
for stardom through high school, tested and honed and
toughened through college. You become overwhelmed by
the victories and the status. You may not even realize it,
but you're not a normal person, you can't be a normal
person, not even in your home. You are forced to play a

role. A part of you becomes what others think of you. You're admired wherever you go, but only for what you represent and not for what you are. But then, what *are* you? Good things come easy to you. You are constantly extolled in the press. It may be the same nonsense written over and over, but you begin to look for it, you keep saying, "Yes, sir" to reporters just to show how polite you are. You're very big at parties, you're almost never alone, you travel in packs, mostly with your teammates because football teams are like tight families. "A man's man," girls will describe you, and though they'll be endlessly frustrated by your reluctance to care deeply for them, their availability is never in doubt. Your days and nights are built around easy gratifications and the search for pleasure. You're never sad, or at least you never show it. Everybody tells you how good you have it, how life is your oyster. Your prospects are the best, there's nothing you can't accomplish, all you have to do is set your mind to it and you'll get there.

It's a big deal, all right. Throughout your impressionable years, you're on display. Even though some of it was a rough go, you spend almost all of your time enjoying the fruits of your triumphs. You want that. Lots of fun and games, a million laughs.

What had I really learned in those four years? Nothing.

My postgraduate existence began with auspicious stupidity. Early in July I went to Minneapolis to meet with the Viking organization and the press. "Rentzel, boy capitalist . . . sounds and looks like a comic-strip athletic prodigy. . . . He swept into town with a million-dollar smile and large blue eyes, one of five Viking newcomers being presented to their public. . . ." The article ran on for about six paragraphs, all about me, mentioning the names of the other four only at the end. It wasn't the sort of thing that would endear me to my new teammates.

I went up to Bemidji, Minnesota, where the Vikings had their training camp, and checked in before heading to Chicago, where I was going to play with the College All-Stars. I had a day to kill and nothing much to do. I thought it would be a good idea to show up at the All-Star camp with a suntan, so I sat under a sun lamp and systematically toasted myself, front, back, sides. I'd never done this before, and I stayed under much longer than I should have. That night I woke up in severe pain.

The next morning Van Brocklin took one look at my beet red body and burst out laughing. He sent me to the hospital, where I was covered with a special ointment, and off I went to Chicago.

Coach Otto Graham took one look at my grease-covered body and winced.

"You belong in a circus," he said.

I'd made a big decision about my football career. I told Otto I wanted to be a receiver in the pros. I'd been a halfback all my life, and I loved carrying the ball. But I enjoyed catching it and running in the open field even more. Besides, it's safer to be a receiver. Most of the time you're out of reach of the linebackers, who are unquestionably the meanest bastards in America.

We were training at Evanston, Illinois, with three weeks to put a team together before the game against the World's Champion Cleveland Browns. There was a lot of talent on that field: Bob Hayes, Fred Biletnikoff, Ralph Neely, Dick Butkus, Jack Snow, Roger Staubach, Gale Sayers, Tucker Frederickson, to name a few. There were also some pretty good guys who knew how to hit the streets at night. Naturally I gravitated toward the best. It was here that I began my friendship with Craig Morton.

It would be difficult to describe the impact he had on me. Nobody I'd ever met was as fun-loving or flamboyant as Craig. And nobody even came close to his capacity to get in some hilarious kind of trouble.

Because of Craig, I began my professional career on the wrong foot. I have no doubt that he would say the same thing about my influence on him—but he'd be lying.

He was an inspiration to my long-dormant powers of violating rules without detection. Like the eleven o'clock curfew. If you were caught missing curfew, you had to go through Otto's "whistle drill," a series of superstrenuous exercises and sprints designed to teach you how to resist temptation the next time. Obviously it was to be avoided at all costs. So I immediately checked out the hotel and found an exit that led to a back alley, where the coaches wouldn't see us leaving.

The evenings, then, were divided into two acts. Act one preceded the eleven o'clock curfew and ended with a quick return for bed check. Act two was the big one, starting with the sneak-out via our secret escape route, and then another ride to Chicago and our waiting companions.

Almost every night it was wine, women, and song. I don't know why for sure, but Otto Graham liked us. He knew what was going on, but he didn't seem to mind as long as he didn't catch us. I think that's because Craig and I worked hard in practice, no matter how tired we were.

But it was inevitable that the odds would catch up to us. One night a hotel employee saw us leave, and he went in and told one of the coaches that a couple of the players had gone out the back way. The first thing the coach did was check our room. It was the whistle drill for the dynamic duo.

The word spread like wildfire. You couldn't have drawn a bigger crowd on that hot July afternoon if you'd offered free beer. The whole team and a fascinated public was there to watch the end of a reign. We were going to be living proof that crime does not pay.

Another challenge to my resourcefulness. During practice I came up with a plan: since the coach would drive us only to exhaustion, obviously one of us should begin to fake exhaustion, leading the other to do the same, in this way convincing Otto that he'd punished us enough. Then, when it was over, we'd get up and run into the locker room like two invincible supermen.

We drew lots and I was to be the actor.

And so it began, immediately after the workout. The field was cleared for the action. Our teammates sat on the sideline, cheering us on and making bets on who would drop first. Since receivers run more than anyone else, most of the money was on me. They were in for a surprise.

Otto opened with a command for a hundred yards of front somersaults. This was followed by four hundred-yard sprints, back and forth. Then fifteen minutes of push-ups, sit-ups, grass drills. Another few hundred-yard sprints. I was beginning to tire and was almost ready to go into my act. Then Otto ordered us to roll on our sides for the length of the field. I started rolling with my arms pinned to my sides, and it wasn't long before I got dizzy. I'd never done this before, but Craig had: he knew enough to roll on raised elbows, thereby making the circumference of the roll larger, covering the same ground without spinning so fast. I began to roll all over the field, unable to keep straight, increasing the dizziness even more. When I got to the end, Otto was waiting, and he ordered us to somersault back. I was as sick as a dog and as white as a ghost, but I made it somehow. I could barely stand and was about to throw up. Another one-hundred-yard sprint, and I was dead. I sank to one knee, unable to move. Otto came up to me, a big grin on his face. He had found out about our plot earlier.

"I know you're faking, but I admire excellence in any form. That was an Oscar-winning performance. Go on in."

But I felt so bad, I couldn't even get up. Otto thought I was still acting and told me I didn't have to keep it up, he wasn't going to run me anymore. I stayed out there for ten minutes, the only one left on the field, trying to collect the strength to go back into the locker room where the players were waiting to congratulate me. They thought I was faking, too. I practically crawled in. The mighty had, indeed, fallen.

The All-Star game was something else again. I devoted the last four days before the game to resting and thinking about football for a change. I practiced hard, studied my plays, and, most important, got some sleep. By game time I was ready. It was a tremendous feeling, playing with so many great athletes, in front of a huge crowd and a national TV audience. And there, across the field, was my first football hero, the great Jim Brown.

An experience like that can be terribly intimidating. The pros have an aura of greatness about them. They handle themselves with tremendous confidence. A college kid facing them cannot help feeling insecure. You line up against them thinking that they're really laughing at you, that every move you could possibly make they've seen a hundred times. When you take off on a pass route, you hear footsteps all around you and you wonder if someone is going to take the ball right out of your hands.

They beat us, all right, 24-16, but we looked good losing, especially in the second half. And I had a particularly good day, leading both teams in receptions, catching one touchdown and almost breaking for another. I didn't disappoint Otto Graham, and most of all I didn't disappoint myself.

Meanwhile, the pro teams had been in training camp for three weeks and were ready to start the preseason. The NFL coaches have mixed feelings about the All-Star game.

Their top rookies miss several weeks of practice and meetings, and the other rookies are way ahead of them in adjusting to the pro system. Frequently, a good prospect is injured and arrives in camp unable to play. If it's tough on the coaches who are eager to evaluate the high draft picks, it is many times more difficult on the rookie himself, who has the major adjustments to make, the most to learn, the most to lose.

I didn't care about all that. I enjoyed the All-Star game enormously. It was the high point of my college career, and it made me feel confident that I could handle myself in any competition. I looked forward to playing for Norm Van Brocklin. I really didn't see how anything could stop me.

Lance Rentzel, pro.

VI

I arrived at Bemidji, Minnesota, and the Vikings gave me a warm welcome. There were a few veterans, Tommy Mason for example, who even came up and introduced themselves. I didn't decorate my room with fancy furniture or hang college awards on the wall, and nobody called me Golden Boy or Wonderbaby or went out of his way to bust my ass to teach me a lesson.

Nonetheless, inside of a week or so I saw I was in for trouble again. I worked hard, but I had a lot to learn, and I started the season playing only on the kicking teams. And Van Brocklin, it turned out, was not the easiest coach in the world to get along with.

He had an excellent football mind, but he believed in motivating players by fear of punishment. He had the sharpest tongue I'd ever confronted. If you had a bad day, he'd let you know about it afterward, especially when we looked at the films, where everyone could see your mistakes. A picture is worth a thousand words, but Van Brocklin liked to supplement it with a few choice comments of his own.

I guess I've got a thin skin. I'm sensitive to severe criticism, largely because I'm my own severest critic. Van Brocklin intimidated me. It didn't make me play better, it only got me down, ending up in a sort of vicious circle: "Rentzel, you're awful!" he would say. I would feel shaky and play a lousy game, thus completing the self-fulfilling prophecy.

Also he didn't like my way of life. He pegged me as a perennial playboy. He got very mad about a party we had one night, one of those spur-of-the-moment get-togethers that sometimes turn out so well. Tommy Mason, who played the guitar, came over to my apartment, where I had a small Hammond organ, and we started playing along with some records. There were a lot of airline stewardesses where I lived, and some of them, hearing the music, came over to see what was happening. A few of our teammates, seeing the girls walking by, dropped in to investigate. One thing led to another, and pretty soon there was a wild party going on. We all had a fine time and, of course, it lasted far too long. The next day Van Brocklin was angry at the partying and blamed me for it. "All you care about is having a good time, Rentzel. I'd trade your ass if anyone would take you!"

Not long afterward, we played Baltimore in the first game of the season. It was a big game because the Colts, as well as the Vikings, were the preseason favorites to win the Western Conference. Van Brocklin wanted to win quite badly. We were favored, but we lost, 35–16, and he was disgusted with all of us. I hadn't played, except to return

108

kickoffs and punts, and I wasn't a factor in the outcome.

In the locker room, before the press was allowed in, Van Brocklin chewed out the whole team. Most of the players tried to be as inconspicuous as possible, but I sat on a taping table in clear view of the coach, unaware of the risk I was taking. He spotted me and took out all his frustrations on me because I had been such a disappointment to him. "And you, Rentzel—you fucking Joe College," he yelled. "I don't know why we ever drafted you." ("Joe College" became my nickname for the rest of the season.) I learned that day to stay out of Van Brocklin's sight after a loss.

I had a lot of trouble because of my image. It was just the way I was, and I became resigned to that after a time. I always enjoyed a little outside companionship. I couldn't weather a training camp without proper relaxation. But the problem was, my evenings would always end up in a furious rush to make curfew.

One night I was hurrying back to the dorms and ran a yellow light. A cop stopped me, and although he didn't give me a ticket, it took precious minutes and I arrived late.

We had a four-story dorm, with rookies on the top floor. To get to the stairway, I had to go right by Van Brocklin's room. I came in as quietly as I could, but the coach had good ears. I heard him coming out, so I ran to the stairs. He came out after me, but just as he'd be about to see me, I'd be rounding a corner for the next flight of stairs. I was quick enough to beat him to the top floor and went flying into my room. The door was open, since it was a hot night, and I dived into bed and pulled the covers over me.

Van Brocklin was no dummy, and he came straight to my room, though I knew he hadn't seen me come into it.

"Rentzel," he said. "Was that you who just came in?"

I stirred, opened my eyes like a man who'd been awakened from a deep sleep, and mumbled, "What . . . what . . .?"

He reached down and jerked the covers off me.

Long, dismal silence. Always ready for any emergency, I came up with a real winner: "Coach—I'll bet you're wondering why I sleep with my clothes on. . . ."

"That'll cost you a hundred," he said.

A game with San Francisco later on in the year was another disaster. I've never seen so many things go wrong in one afternoon. It was a very cold day in Minneapolis (the chill factor was well below zero), and the field was completely frozen. Dave Osborn fumbled the opening kickoff and San Francisco recovered, converting it into a field goal. I dropped the ensuing kickoff, recovered it, ran another ten yards, got hit, and fumbled again. Two fumbles on one play, a rare feat. Frisco ended up with another three points. The game had just started and we were lucky to be trailing by only six points.

They kicked to me again, and for a second it looked as if I would go all the way. I imagined myself crossing the goal line and a feeling of triumph came over me. Suddenly I was hit from nowhere. I looked around in disbelief and realized that Dave Osborn had accidentally knocked me down, trying to block the only 49er who was near. As Dave and I came off the field, Van Brocklin snarled, "It looks like a goddamn three-ring circus out there."

Tommy Mason replaced Osborn at safety for the next kickoff. He backed into the goalpost just as he was about to catch the ball, and it bounced off his chest. He was momentarily stunned and I barely recovered it before San Francisco did. Some of the fans started booing. (They hadn't seen anything yet.)

Later on in the game, I fair caught a punt on our own four-yard line. It was an extremely stupid play, due to poor communication between the other safety and me. The boos grew louder.

I came off the field, put on my warm-up jacket and backed up close to the infrared heater on the sideline. The next thing I knew, my jacket was on fire. Some of the other players had to come over and help me put it out. The fans cheered—they thought that was more exciting than the game.

The worst was yet to come. The next-to-last kickoff was a short one, and I decided to catch it on the fly. On a frozen field, it is usually best to play it safe: let the ball hit the ground and then pick it up. But I believe in gambling, especially when you need to do something spectacular to get out of the doghouse. I always was a bad gambler. Just as I was about to field the ball, I slipped on the ice. I went flying feet first and the ball went over my head. I got up and recovered it just in time. The fans went wild—and so did Van Brocklin. When I came off the field, he was there to meet me. I've had friendlier greetings.

The final kickoff was deep in the end zone. I just caught it and went down on one knee. It was an automatic touchback and the ball went out to the twenty-yard line. Even though it was a very routine play, the fans were so pleased that nothing went wrong, they gave me an ovation when I came off. It was a perfect touch of sarcasm, and I got the message.

Surprisingly enough, we won the game.

The following Tuesday, we watched the game films. The kicking game was on a separate reel, so all my bad plays flashed on the screen one after the other. Everyone cracked up. I laughed too—but you can't enjoy it as much when you're the big joke. Van Brocklin never said a word. He just kept repeating those plays over and over, embarrassing me that much more. Finally he turned off the projector, switched on the lights, and said, "You know, Rentzel—you ought to be an All-Rookie." It really surprised me. I wasn't expecting a comment like that and I thought maybe he was trying to give me a little encouragement. So I said, "Thanks, Coach." Then he added, "Yeah—All-Rookie fuck-up." He switched off the lights, turned on the projector, and never said another word. That really broke up the place.

Several weeks later, we played Baltimore again. We had come back from that opening loss, and a victory would have tied us for the league lead. In the fourth quarter Baltimore was ahead, but we still had a good chance to win. I took care of that, in my own inimitable way. I fumbled a kick, and the Colts recovered. I knew Van Brocklin would be waiting for me and I wanted to avoid him. Baltimore's bench was on the same side of the field as ours, so I went off with their players and stayed where he couldn't see me. He was frantically looking for me, pushing players aside trying to find out where I was.

Baltimore scored, putting the game out of reach. I went back on the field the same way I had left. Van Brocklin didn't spot me until the Colts were almost ready to kick off. Even though I was over fifty yards away, that didn't stop him—he had to say something. He cupped his hands and yelled, "Let's see what you can fuck up now, Rentzel." A lot of people heard him besides me.

Needless to say, that didn't fill me with confidence. As the ball came down, I thought, "What in the hell's going to happen to me now?" But for once everything went right. I ran 101 yards for a touchdown, which I think is still a Viking record. It was the perfect squelch for Van Brocklin.

Suddenly, I was his boy—until after the next game. I started on offense, but played poorly and finished the season on the bench.

112

I came to realize that I have the kind of personality that coaches do not appreciate. I'm simply not the kind of player who lives football twenty-four hours a day. I prepare myself to play in my own way, concentrating on football at practices and meetings and then, very intensely, at games. At other times I relax and enjoy myself. I smile a lot, I'm fun-loving and gregarious, I don't even get nervous and tense before a game the way most guys do. All this is sometimes interpreted as indifference, especially since this image of me is continually reinforced by those stories about the playboy rich kid who could buy himself a team if he wished. Because pro football is a team game, coaches want everything to be regimented; nothing must jar that endless appeal for all ballplayers to "give 110 percent effort." The ideal player is a somber guy, preferably married, who hardly ever speaks except to say "Yes, sir," and who does nothing but think about football. If he has a bad day, well, that's only human. If a guy like me has a bad day, it's because of my attitude. As Van Brocklin had put it, I was a "Joe College."

But there was no bitterness between Van Brocklin and me. We laughed a lot together (usually off the field), and many times he was as enjoyable a person to be around as I had ever met. He only bothered me when he was in a bad mood. His moods were either good or bad—never in between. Undoubtedly, he would have been in better spirits around me if I had been playing better. He had a right to be disappointed. I was not helping the team very much. The respect of my teammates is the most important thing in athletics to me, and it was evident that it would be lacking until I made a valid contribution.

It was an unsatisfying season for me, but in spite of my errors, I had made a certain amount of progress. The Vikings had a good wide receiver named Paul Flatley, and I learned by watching him. I also picked up a lot of things

113

by studying outstanding receivers from other teams, usually on film. I started to imitate all of their moves, but this proved to be a mistake. What was good for someone else wasn't necessarily good for me. But out of it I developed my own style, my own way of doing things. In the pros, unlike college, you play against the same guys week after week, year after year. You get to know the way they defend you, you learn to analyze their moves, and you begin to work accordingly. I did a great deal of thinking about that in the off-season.

So when I returned for my second year, I was definitely not depressed by my prospects. I came back lighter and quicker than before. I had gotten myself into top shape and was eager to play.

I had a fine exhibition season and was going to start on offense in the opener against San Francisco. Then, three days before the game, I sprained my ankle badly in practice.

Back into the doghouse.

It was very depressing. I wanted to be a winner for the club, and now I had to spend all my time in the whirlpool. "The S.S. *Rentzel*," they called it. Sound-ray therapy, heat lamps, and incessant limping. I was no good to anybody, least of all myself.

I happened to pick up a book in the training room one day and read it. It was George Orwell's *1984,* and it had a tremendous effect on me. Sometimes you can read something at a time when you're supersensitive, and it becomes doubly upsetting as a result. The book pulled me a thousand miles away from my problems with the Vikings and sent me spinning into another world. It shook my faith in religion and fed all my growing cynicism about human nature. There were references in the novel about how God was merely a ruse, created by powerful men to keep the powerless in their place, a political force to prevent rebelliousness. It showed how man would become willing to submit to authority, Big Brother, and permit his life to be organized and regimented into a totalitarian, technocratic, computerized society. And though the hero learns he has to resist, the power of the book was in the tyranny of the system that the people were living under—and I could not escape the feeling that Orwell's predictions were all terribly valid.

Experiences like that aren't pleasant, but it wouldn't have been so bad if I had been playing football and contributing something to the team. Instead, I felt like a burden, nothing more than a cripple for all practical purposes.

I began to feel sorry for myself. I suddenly felt I had too few good friends, and my personal life wasn't any better. I had broken up with Marcia a few months before, primarily because I wasn't ready to get married. She felt our relationship was getting nowhere, and she wanted out. I guess it was the only solution, but I missed her. I was afraid of Van Brocklin and hated the prospect of facing him daily when I couldn't even practice. The trainers said the sprain would heal quickly enough, and that buoyed me up, but when I tried to run on it a week or so later, the pain was excruciating. I started going out at night, primarily because I couldn't sleep anyway, I was too restless and frustrated. It only served to make me all the more tired, depleting my strength and making me more vulnerable emotionally. Then, too, my mother went into the hospital for surgery; we feared a malignancy, and that frightened the hell out of me—especially with her family history.

It was the end of September, 1966. I left practice, tired, frustrated, depressed. . . . I had actually been nursing thoughts about quitting football, about quitting immediately, in time to return to school and get my master's degree in math. I was confused about what my purpose in life ought to be, suddenly wondering if football really wasn't that important in the overall scheme of things, that if we were all heading for 1984, what sort of stupidity kept me playing football as though I were just another automaton? . . .

I drove past a park, and there I saw two young girls. . . .

VII

What had I done?

I knew and I didn't know. As I was driving away from practice, I had a strange sensation of detachment. I had no idea where I was going or why. I just drove. I could never explain how I felt, it was a childish mood more than anything else. When I was a kid I'd sometimes run up to a doorbell, push it, then run away. Why does a kid do a thing like that? He doesn't even stay to see the door opened and the look of bewilderment on the person's face. But it's satisfying because he has *done something,* silly as it is, silly as he *knows* it is. I'd played many similar tricks when I was a certain age, perhaps eleven or twelve. On this Thursday in September, feeling useless to everyone and to myself as well, maybe I needed to be a child again, to thumb my nose at the teacher when her back was turned and get the rest of the class laughing. Or maybe I needed something much deeper than that, some proof and reassurance as a man.

I was never attracted to little girls, except when I was a little boy. In adult life I had no special sexual desires for women younger than myself. I never had dreams about them, I don't think I've even spoken to very many little girls since I was that age myself. On this day, for some reason, I needed someone to play with me in a childish game I was making up. Look at me, look at me. Look at what I've got. I sat in the car and they came over and I exposed myself. It took maybe ten seconds; then I drove off, strangely relieved.

I drove back to my apartment, lost in other depressing thoughts. I had put the incident right out of my mind. It wasn't amnesia; I could remember doing it if my mind turned to the recollection, but my mind turned away from it. A most peculiar thing had happened to me, and not for the first time. Yet I had no thoughts or feelings about it whatsoever.

Apparently I have a well-developed ability to resist facing what I don't wish to face. I know, everybody can do that to some degree, but I happen to be accomplished at it. I can really turn things off. Anything. Well, almost anything. I don't brood about things for long. I'll play music. Keep busy. Kid around with friends. Have fun with girls. Go out to a club. Meet people. Talk. Yes, talk. I am usually gregarious, even when I'm going through a difficult period. I can turn myself on with my own energies. I am good at making merry when I have to. It doesn't solve anything, I know that too, it just gets me through the night. The way I figured it, I'd have to face tomorrow anyway, I might as well make the best of the end of today.

I didn't completely forget what I had done, though I wished I could. I was ashamed of it, no doubt of that. The

118

secret memory lay inside me for days, like some indigestible meal, gradually fading in time. It was there, but outside my conscious thoughts.

Thus in a way I was genuinely startled when Van Brocklin called me into his office the following week and confronted me with a police report. I didn't lie to him, but I avoided admitting the truth. That was good enough for him, he seemed relieved, and he started to laugh. He was embarrassed, a little ill at ease, sure, but he was also amused. He wasn't being cruel or anything. I guess he thought I was the last guy in the world who would do such a thing. He just couldn't believe it. In a way, that helped me, it made it seem that maybe it really hadn't happened at all, that it was part of some dream world that I was living in. And then, the following day and the next, he'd joke about it. He'd call me "Flasher" and then laugh at me, and I'd laugh with him, make a big joke out of it, for no one knew what he meant by it at the time.

On Sunday, we went down to Dallas to play the Cowboys; I was only returning kickoffs and punts, I wasn't a regular yet, but that was enough: on the opening kickoff, I got hit hard, high and low, reinjuring my ankle. I stayed in the game, but I was limping noticeably, and Van Brocklin, in obvious disgust, finally took me out in the second quarter.

I brooded on the plane coming home, my foot packed in ice. Any athlete knows how a bad injury can be as devastating mentally as it is physically. Even when it heals, and that takes time, a player often becomes preoccupied with the injured area. You lose confidence, you think more about the injury than you do about your assignment. If you're an unproven player, you eventually lose the respect of your teammates if they feel you're hurt too often. They lose faith in your value to the club. You're spending all your time in the whirlpool. "You can't make the club in the tub," they say. They come to regard you as a prima donna, and soon you're ignored.

As I sat in that plane, I wondered what my teammates were thinking of me.

The next day, Jim Finks, the Vikings' general manager, called me into his office to tell me the news: I had been positively identified and charges were being pressed against me.

"Well . . . ?" he said.

I looked at him and I couldn't talk. He was one of those wonderful men you meet every so often: tough, fair, completely honorable. You would have to be crazy not to have complete respect for him. He was asking me if I did it, and I couldn't tell him. As with Van Brocklin, I couldn't tell him yes and I couldn't tell him no. I would make up an answer that would come off like a question, and he would ask something else or try to answer it himself. But I was in trouble now, and he needed a definite answer.

Finally, I admitted it. Yes, it was me. It was true. He had to know it, and I had to face it.

Jim Finks said he would do everything he could for me. He brought in a highly respected lawyer named Sid Goff, who sent me to two psychiatrists for examination and evaluation. For one thing, he wanted to show the court that I was seeking help, and for another, he wanted me to get help.

The psychiatrists were the first I'd ever talked with. I told them everything I could about what had happened to me that afternoon, but I spoke from the point of view that there was nothing really wrong with me. I just couldn't get myself to understand that I was sick in some way, that what I had done was really part of a deep, mysterious neurosis. They listened and we talked, and in the end they agreed with me: it was a momentary aberration resulting from the stress I was under. They did not feel that I had a serious emotional problem or that I needed further psychiatric help. Naturally I accepted their decision. Indeed, I had worked for it. All very stupid, of course, knowing that I was actually deceiving them—and worst of all, deceiving myself.

As it turned out, everyone combined to perpetuate the deception.

Mother: When I heard about it from Lance, certain things he said convinced me that he was protecting a married woman he knew—that she was in his room at the motel at the time of the incident, and that he could not clear himself without involving her. . . . Nothing could have made me believe he did it. I knew his moral values, his deep religious conviction. He couldn't be sick, I reasoned, or somewhere, sometime, as close as we were as a family, someone would have seen some abnormality. The only abnormal thing about Lance was his great talent—musical, physical, and mental, and how hard he has worked all his life to perfect these talents. He has never given us anything but pride and pleasure since the day he came into the world. If he could do this thing, then anybody can do anything.

Since charges had been pressed against me, I had to go down one morning to the St. Paul police station to be booked. I had never been inside one before, and I had no idea what to expect. It was like a gangster movie, the suspect getting fingerprinted and mug shots taken. I'll never forget the feeling I had. It couldn't be happening to me, but it was, and I was ashamed of it. I'd never live it down, it was as if I'd put on a mask and suddenly I was a criminal, and the cops were staring at me with a very cold look, professionally cold: they had seen just about everything before, but who was this nut to add to their list? At the time in Minnesota, I wasn't much of a ballplayer, no one recognized me around there, it was all very impersonal. Still, I was scared, I couldn't help that, I was feeling crushed inside, but I was struggling not to appear that way, I just didn't want to let anyone think I was guilty of anything. So I tried to make light of it all, it was a routine thing of some kind, and when they took my picture, I said something to the photographer, like "Hey, should I smile?" and he didn't say a word, not a word, and so I had to add to it, "If they turn out good, I'd like to order a dozen," and finally someone laughed and someone else smiled and I smiled and pretty soon it was over with.

Sure. But I left a piece of myself in that police station.

It was a quiet scene in St. Paul, October, 1966, when the judge gave his decision on my case. He leaned over the bench and spoke so low, it was almost impossible to hear him. It was only when I heard that a reporter from the *Minneapolis Tribune* was there that I understood the judge's compassion. He was trying to keep the matter private.

They had reduced the charge against me to disorderly conduct and left me free to go. Nobody said a word to me one way or another; I simply returned to the Vikings to play the remainder of the season.

Still, I worried about the press. I hated the thought of seeing this thing brought out into the open, of seeing my reputation smeared in print, of having to face my teammates, the girls I was dating, of knowing that my family would hear of it. Later that day, I stood around the lobby of the Holiday Inn where I was staying, waiting for the

122

afternoon papers to arrive. I bought the first copy available and went to my room, scanning the front page, the second, then the sports pages. Nothing. Not a word. I couldn't believe it, it was too good to be true. I started at the beginning again, carefully this time. Page by page. I'd seen my name in the papers hundreds of times for the last eight years of my life and I knew how to look for it, and this was the first time I didn't want to see it, I prayed not to see it, and the more I went through the paper, the happier I became.

Until I got to the back page, where the nightly TV programs were listed, to be seen and read only by people who wondered what TV shows they were going to watch that night—which, in St. Paul and Minneapolis, was practically everybody.

VIKINGS RENTZEL

PLEADS GUILTY TO DISORDERLY CHARGE

Thomas Lance Rentzel, a 22 yr. old halfback for the Minnesota Vikings football team, pleaded guilty Tuesday in St. Paul Municipal Court to a charge of disorderly conduct.

Rentzel was charged in a complaint issued by the St. Paul Police Department with having exposed himself to small children two weeks ago in the St. Paul's Highland Park area.

Judge James Lynch ordered Rentzel, who is single, to seek psychiatric care. He ordered that a psychiatric report be forwarded to the court, stating whether Rentzel might repeat the acts.

I read it once, I read it twice—and then I let out a terrible cry. I had never felt anything like that before, the pain within me was indescribable.

As it turned out, I was not taken handcuffed through the

streets to be pilloried by mobs of screaming indignant parents.

I was not put on trial before the judgment of my peers and found guilty of my crime.

I was not chastized by the Viking management or vilified by my coach or my teammates.

I was in no way subjected to suspension or punishment or even criticism by officials of the National Football League.

Except for the humiliating publicity, I was not made to feel guilty or forced to suffer the consequences of my act. In effect, it was not a whole lot worse than if I'd been caught speeding, then managed to beat the rap.

With hindsight, this was probably the worst solution possible, for it permitted me to sweep my problems under the rug.

. . . During my years of coaching, I had the opportunity to work with many fine young men. As a coach, one develops closer relationships with players than is usually the case in normal professor-student associations. I can say unequivocally that Lance Rentzel ranks among the finest young men I have ever known. . . . It is totally inconceivable to me that he could have been guilty of the charges that have been made. . . .

Charles B. (Bud) Wilkinson

It is impossible for us who have known him these many years to understand how his name has become involved in any disorderly or indecent action, and we can remain but incredulous.

G. Raymond Campbell
Westminster Presbyterian Church,
Oklahoma City

... Lance is known as an intelligent, devoted, and moral young man who is proud of his home and parentage.... I feel that he is trustworthy in all respects. ...

George L. Cross
President, University of Oklahoma

I have known his family even more years than I have known Lance.... It is inconceivable to me that Lance could have been guilty of the charges made, and there is nothing I know of over the years that would indicate in any way anything but a high moral character and a young man dedicated to a pathway of honorable and outstanding performance in all fields. ...

Mike Monroney
United States Senate

Lance has never been anything but a pleasure to us from the day he was born. It is inconceivable to us, or to anyone who has ever known Lance, that he would be guilty of *any* form of disorderly conduct, and certainly not a sex offense. His whole life has been a model that other youngsters strive to emulate. He neither smokes nor drinks—beyond an occasional beer. He has never been involved in any sort of trouble. The fact that he has pled guilty does not alter our faith in him. ...

Mr. and Mrs. Delos Rentzel

None of the people close to me could believe there was anything wrong with me. That made it easier for me to deny it to myself.

Still, I had to live with my embarrassments. Like the confrontation with my teammates at practice, the day after the story came out in the papers. When I walked into the locker room, everyone was getting dressed, but they all stopped what they were doing to look at me. Paul Dickson, not one of my favorite vets, especially when he got drunk and gave me sarcastic advice on how to make it as a pro, made some smart-ass remarks. A few of my friends walked over and said sympathetic things, but most of them figured it would embarrass me if they said anything, so they kept away. It was a very difficult twenty minutes.

I walked alone to the meeting room down a long concrete corridor that seemed like the last mile. Outwardly, as always, I suppose I didn't appear nervous; but inwardly I was fighting a great battle. Although I didn't have to say anything to them, I felt they deserved some sort of explanation. Yet, if I told the truth, I was afraid they would reject me completely. I settled it by talking briefly and skirting the issue. I wanted to confide in them completely, but all I could say was: "You know, this is a very complicated situation. I hope you guys will understand. You don't know me very well and I know I've let you down, so I can't ask for any special degree of consideration. Just believe that there's more to it than what appeared in the paper. I hope that you will still think of me as part of the team."

I wanted to end on a lighter note, so I said, "Maybe I need a better press agent." It was said with a smile, and I thought they would realize I was just trying to break the tension. I meant that I wanted them to treat me just the same as before. But they didn't laugh or smile or even react to the statement, except to look at me in dead silence. Obviously they didn't understand the way I had intended it. I regretted saying that for a long time to come.

The balance of the season was almost a total waste, both on the field and off. I became reluctant to go out at night. I hated the looks I got in restaurants; all it took was one person to recognize me, and there would be all those nudges and whispers and stares. I came to hate them, hearing nothing but knowing exactly what they were saying. One of the girls I was seeing used to add to my depression by telling me all the rumors that were spreading around. One of them was that I'd been caught in a shower with a bunch of children. Others were even wilder. I tried to keep calm about all the talk, but it was too much to take. I remember one night when I really wanted to be with her, to enjoy her company in some quiet way, and she was just bursting to tell me the latest dirt she had heard. It ruined everything. Sometimes I thought that people in town just didn't have enough to talk about. I should have realized that bad news—especially when it's dirty—always drives out the good.

Jim Finks was sympathetic and concerned. Right after the publicity first broke, he offered to trade me to another team if I felt it would help me psychologically. I declined, thinking that it would be better to stay with the Vikings, get well, and play good ball. It was the only thing I knew how to do. Running away from Minneapolis was not the answer. I wanted to come through it with a certain amount of self-respect.

I kept trying to work my ankle back into shape, running harder each week and spending more time getting treatment. I practiced as hard as I could to show Van Brocklin that I wasn't giving up on myself. I didn't kid around very much, not only as a tactic but because I didn't feel inclined to. I was strictly a football player, and I eventually won a starting spot on offense.

We were playing the Detroit Lions, a tough team, and I was primed to prove that I belonged in the starting lineup. In the first quarter, however, I broke a pass pattern and caused Tarkenton to throw an interception. That was all I needed; in that one play I lost any chance I had of gaining Fran's confidence. I didn't blame him; a quarterback never has faith in a receiver until he's proven himself in crucial situations. Practice and preseason games mean little. It's what a man does when it counts that matters.

After the game I was reminded of this as I came out of the locker room. A kid walked up and asked me to sign his autograph book. I had just finished writing "Lance" when he saw Fran. He jerked the pen out of my hand, then grabbed his book and ran over to get Fran's autograph. It didn't do much for my ego, but I admired the kid's honesty.

Anyway, I spent the rest of the season on the bench, and after the last game I asked Jim Finks to trade me. It hadn't been an easy decision for me, for it demonstrated neither pride nor gratitude. I simply couldn't see myself coming back for another try, a try that would probably end in failure, as the previous efforts had. And I didn't particularly want to play in Minnesota. I had come to hate the cold, the frozen fields. I was paranoid about my notoriety there. I knew that a change would be the best thing for me.

Again Jim was good to me. He even asked where I would like to go, in case it could be arranged. I'd thought a lot about that, and my answer was Dallas. I lived there in the off-season. They had a championship-caliber team, and they needed a receiver. He said he would try. He promised me that, and I knew he would. He was that kind of man.

(condensed)
October 28, 1966

Dear Lance,

. . . Nothing is as little heeded as unsolicited advice. A little boy once wrote a theme—"Socrates was a Greek philosopher who went about giving people good advice. They made him drink poison."

Nevertheless, you have been so much in my

thoughts recently that I want to mention a few things I hope you will consider.

You are a man of great and varied talent . . . your own breadth of ability makes it difficult for you to come to firm grip with your future. . . . Your competitive spirit burns brightly—and while you've "made it" into Pro Football, you haven't yet achieved stardom. It is only natural that you wish to clear this final hurdle.

However, time passes and men and the world change. Your ultimate happiness will depend almost entirely on the joy you take in your work—your productivity—during your mature years. To delay getting on with this most important part of your life—in the interest of one more athletic honor—is, in my opinion, questionable judgment. . . . There is no limit on what you can do. Your only problem is to ascertain what activities give you the greatest sense of creative joy.

You have the ability to do whatever you choose. . . . It remains my hope that you will begin to evaluate life's varied opportunities so that as a mature man you are prepared to contribute to life in a manner worthy of your God-given talents.

Most sincerely,
Bud Wilkinson

VIII

I spent Christmas, 1966, with my parents in Oklahoma City and then flew to Dallas, where Craig Morton and I had decided to share an apartment. As I saw it, the setting was perfect for me: I had some good friends in Dallas, and my troubles had not been in the papers there. I went out to watch the Cowboys practice for the NFL Championship game against Green Bay. They were an impressive team, and I began to fantasize about playing for them the next year. I could even picture myself in a Cowboy uniform.

A couple of days later I was in the uniform of the Air National Guard.

I had joined in the spring but was allowed to take my basic training after the season ended. I was ordered to report to Lackland Air Force Base in San Antonio on December 27. Naturally I arrived at the last legal minute for induction to begin a service career that served to inspire only a desire to get out of every possible duty. If the military doesn't get you shot in a war, it can almost as easily bore you to death. I had faced enough shit in my time to know what it was all about, but I quickly realized that this was going to be an enlightening experience. It took over four hours to be processed through the induction center, owing to the tedious paper work. I kept looking at this big sign: "Welcome to the Air Force." It was an ironic touch to the sudden preposterous change into tyranny the moment after we were sworn in. We went outside and lined up to wait for the buses that would take us to our barracks. Then one guy happened to laugh at somebody's fragile attempt at humor, and the NCO jumped all over us. Bend down and pick up luggage, straighten up, drop luggage, bend down and pick up luggage, straighten up, drop luggage. For an hour. And I was freezing because I was out in twenty-five-degree weather without a warm coat. (I had been told by friends not to take *any* additional clothing.) There I was at four in the morning, cold as hell, doing a ridiculous monotonous exercise over and over, and all I could think of was "Welcome to the Air Force."

The most memorable part of my time there had to do with my hair. On the first day, on command, I had to pay sixty-five cents to have it all cut off. Every bit of it, right down to the scalp. I felt so stripped of my identity (I guess I always did have a Samson complex), I went to the PX and had my pictures taken. Mug shots, police style. I felt as if I were in prison and I wanted pictures to prove it. Then, the following week, it was cut again. The brass wanted total baldness. All my life I'd hated hats, and suddenly I wouldn't go anywhere without one.

I immediately turned my thoughts toward figuring out a way to avoid getting the last haircut, scheduled for the day before my release! I swore that they would never get me. What good would it be to rejoin civilian life without any hair? I considered the possibility of buying a wig, but rejected it; I was not a man who would submit to the system by a compromise of his identity. I was going to beat this system or die.

During the next couple of weeks, I tested various plans, but none of them proved to be foolproof. Then I became friendly with a doctor at the base hospital, who happened to be an avid football fan. I had a broken bone in my hand that had never healed properly, and he offered to fix it—at the government's expense. This was fine with me, if the operation could be performed on the day my squad was scheduled for its last haircut.

"Why not?" he said. Since he was a major, he didn't think there would be any difficulty.

And so it was arranged. Basic training was a depressing experience. I arrived with the attitude that since I was there, I might as well do a good job. But it soon became evident that this point of view was worthless. They were only interested in getting you through your training as quickly as possible, so they could take on the next batch. I therefore developed a more typically military way of looking at things: do what you're told and no more. I was comforted by the knowledge that I would leave with perhaps a quarter inch of hair—which isn't much, I know, but neither is a swallow of water except to a man dying of thirst. Everything is relative.

I might add that I didn't particularly appreciate talking to Craig on the phone and finding out that he was off to Hawaii with a very cute girl I knew, sort of a consolation prize to soothe him after the Cowboys' loss to Green Bay. That may have eased his suffering, but it made mine worse.

Finally, the big day. I went to the hospital and got through the minor operation. I returned to the barracks feeling great. By this time most of the guys in my barracks knew what I'd been up to. And they hoped I would get away with my ruse. They wanted to see somebody fool the establishment just once.

The next day we were standing in line to receive our final paycheck—our last official duty. After that I was home free. A friend of mine from San Antonio was waiting in his car to take me to the airport for a flight to Minneapolis. I inched along, closer and closer to the Promised Land. There were only five guys ahead of me. Then four. Three.

"Rentzel!"

The voice of our drill sergeant was, by then, very familiar. I turned in agony.

"Fall out!" he barked.

He took me to the lieutenant in charge, having found out that I hadn't had my last haircut. The lieutenant wanted to know why. I delivered my excuse, all very legitimate, and was taken to the captain's office, where I was ordered to get the haircut immediately. I was a cornered man, relying on his wits to save him.

"Captain, there are extenuating circumstances. . . ."

"What are they, Rentzel?"

"Well, sir, I'd like permission to speak to the general about this."

"What?"

"Yes, sir, I know it seems trivial, but there's a question of my career at issue."

"Your career!"

"If you don't mind, Captain . . ."

I persevered, and as everyone knows, there are rewards for that quality. I was taken to the general himself.

"You see, sir, I have this Vitalis commercial scheduled in three weeks, and if I don't have any hair, I won't be able to do it. Not only will I lose a lot of money, but the

133

producers will lose faith in me. After all, I did sign a contract and I don't believe in breaking contracts. I think of myself as an honorable man."

He stared at me for a long moment. I could see he was an honorable man. He was wondering if *I* was.

"We have quite a few entertainers come through here, Rentzel. They all get their hair cut, just like everyone else. I don't suppose they like it any more than you, but everyone makes sacrifices in the military."

He stopped there, obviously in doubt about what to say next. I watched him intently, waiting for some sign of mercy. He must have sensed this, for he began to soften.

"I'll tell you what, Rentzel. I'll tell the barber just to trim the sides a bit."

So the sergeant marched me to the barbershop, right past my barracks. Everyone was packing, but they came to the windows when they saw me going by.

"Look at Rentzel, they're taking him to the barber!"

"The poor bastard . . ."

"Shit, they caught him!"

"Hey, Lance. Tough luck!"

"He's smiling. That's what I call guts."

"That poor son of a bitch . . ."

That was the last time I ever saw those guys, and to this day they don't know that I got away with it by the oldest maneuver in the world: I slipped the barber five dollars to go one step beyond the general's orders.

When I returned to Minneapolis to complete my active duty in the Air National Guard, I learned that Jim Finks had been trying to make good on his promise. He had offered me to Tom Landry, Tex Schramm, et al. But they weren't particularly eager to trade for me, and I could understand that. I had played little and showed a tendency toward injury. And I had personal problems too. My only asset was potential.

Yes, Jim Finks tried. Then he became terribly ill. At one time, they didn't know if he would pull through or not. This delayed the negotiations considerably, and things looked bad for both of us. But I worried about Jim much more than myself. I was fighting for a new chance in life. He was fighting for life itself.

In the end, there was a double victory. Jim recovered, and Lance Rentzel was traded to the Cowboys.

May 2, 1967. I'll never forget that date. It was my last day of military duty, and I celebrated with some of my friends at the base. I hadn't known them very long, but I felt they were sincerely happy for me.

I was packed and ready to go within twenty-four hours, that's how fast I wanted to get out of there, how anxious I was to flee the scene of my failures. I left behind few real friends. One was Jim Finks. And another was Norm Van Brocklin.

I came to Dallas in the best of spirits. Opportunity was knocking, and this time I was going to make the most of it. There was absolutely no doubt in my mind about one thing: I would show the Cowboys it was the best trade they had ever made.

IX

I started fast with Dallas in the first scrimmage at training camp. I caught all kinds of passes and ran wild. Give or take a few bad moments, I continued to do so all season long. The Cowboys needed a big fast receiver to complement the amazing Mr. Bob Hayes, and I was there to oblige them. Inspired by this second chance in the pros, liberated from the cold surroundings of Minnesota, I simply caught fire, and it never burned out. The name of the game was confidence. I felt on top of everything. From a third-rate substitute with the Vikings, I became a top NFL pass receiver with 996 yards gained on fifty-eight receptions, a figure bettered by only two players in the league. We ended the regular season with a 9-5 record, nothing sensational, but good enough to win the division championship.

All of this had an exhilarating effect on me. I was an

entirely different person from the one in Minnesota: much more confident, happier, and more relaxed. When I went out for a good time, it was genuinely enjoyed and not for escape or out of desperation. This, finally, was what I thought life was supposed to be like.

I'd wake up laughing and go to bed laughing. In between, there were football, women, friends, a daily package of good times. I also loved music, I had a talent for it, and every so often I'd sit in with some of the groups in town and sing and play till all hours of the night.

The Cowboy management was good to me. They made me feel right at home. All they asked was that I didn't room with Craig in training camp. When I negotiated my contract, I signed it first and told Tex Schramm to fill in whatever amount he thought I was worth. He wrote in $21,000, plus $2,000 more as a bonus if I made the starting team. It was no more than I had made the year before, but the way I figured it, I'd been sadly overpaid at Minnesota. As I told a newspaper interviewer, "All I did with the Vikings was lead the team in injuries."

My problems were minor. I had so much to do, so much to enjoy, I'd sometimes arrive late for practice, or miss curfew now and then. I became known for my freewheeling, fun-loving attitude, but if Coach Landry objected to my tardiness at practice, he had to admit that when I arrived I worked as hard as or harder than anyone else. On Sunday he knew that I could be relied on to be where I was supposed to be, that I would hardly ever miss an assignment, that I would frequently make the big play and rarely make the big mistake. I appreciated the fact that Landry judged my attitude by what I did on the field—not off it.

The Cowboys themselves were tremendous. It was great to be with Craig and Ralph Neely again, and almost immediately I made many new friends. When I first met Don Meredith, he was sitting in front of his locker, exhausted. "The Lord gave me a pitiful body," he said, "but I'll just have to do the best I can with it." He had skinny legs and everyone would kid him about them, but he would kid back, making up bigger jokes about himself than anyone else could. He was also intelligent, he could read defenses well and move the club when he had to. But his biggest asset was his leadership, his ability to inspire his teammates.

Once, early in the season, when we were behind with about a minute to go, he threw me a sideline, a perfect pass for the first down, and I dropped it. I went back to the huddle thinking I had really let him down, and he would lose confidence in me the way Fran Tarkenton had. But he called the exact same play again. I left the huddle knowing I'd make the first down this time, and I did.

In one game, late in the season, he got hit by a big defensive end who jammed his forearm through Don's face mask, completely smashing his nose. They set it back in place that night, taped him up, then put him back on the field for the next game as if nothing had happened. He was one of the gutsiest guys I'd ever seen. He had two bad knees, a bad ankle, broken ribs, his nose was all over his face, but he was still out there playing. And best of all, he really knew how to enjoy himself. I sensed that, underneath it all, he had his share of problems, but they were insignificant compared to his tremendous capacity for life. I learned a lot of football from Don, and we had more than our shares of laughs together.

It was inevitable that I would have problems with Pete Gent, the starting flanker for the previous two years. My trade made him concerned, because he arrived early at training camp, much lighter than usual, and very determined. At first he made it plain that he resented my being there. When it became obvious that I would take his job away from him, he would throw barbs at me whenever he could. But he couldn't sustain such a negative attitude for long because he was actually a tremendously positive guy. He had a clever wit and an extremely quick mind. He was the first player on the club to let his hair grow, and that was no small accomplishment in Dallas. He had a five-minute TV show late at night, and it was really wild. He'd come on dressed up like Abraham Lincoln, beard, stove-pipe hat, but he'd never refer to it, he'd just talk football as though he were dressed perfectly normally.

At midseason Landry changed him to a reserve tight end, using him in long-yardage situations when we had to pass. But a couple of weeks later Bob Hayes got hurt, and Landry decided on the plane back to Dallas that he would move Pete over to split end for the next game. He came back to the players' section and told him, "Pete, I'm going to put you over on the other side this week."

Without blinking an eye, Pete replied, "You mean I'm going to play for Philadelphia?"

Pete was a rebel. He was his own man and he was true to himself. In the end, we became good friends. Landry eventually traded him to the Giants, but they put him on waivers, and he retired soon afterward.

The toughest player of all was Walt Garrison, a true cowboy, the only one on the club. He chewed tobacco, whittled like a master, rode broncos, roped steers. He had his own ranch and loved it. There was no bullshit with him; he, like Pete Gent, was a completely sincere, down-to-earth person. He had a great sense of humor, but with a western flavor to it. If someone was kidding him, which was often, he'd say something like "I'm not like a train, fella, you don't have to pay to get on." He wasn't very big, but put a football in his hands and he was something else. He was one of the most determined runners I'd ever seen. You had to damn near kill him to bring him down. He also had an uncanny sense of balance, so it was rare that one man was able to tackle him. But his most admirable quality was his ability to rise to the occasion. If it was a big game, you knew Walt would be ready.

I remember when we played Cleveland for the Eastern Conference Championship, and we faced a critical situation late in the third quarter, fourth down and two yards to go. Walt hit into a stone wall, bounced off, tried another hole, got hit, bounced back, stayed on his feet with a 260-pound tackle on his back, finally found an opening and fought off another tackle until he could make his yardage for the first down.

"Dammit, Garrison," I said as we huddled up, "if you didn't come to play, why don't you quit and let someone else come in?"

"Keep talkin', big boy," he said, "don't let fear and common sense hold you back."

Then there was Bob Hayes, a man with tremendous talents. He was such a threat to score from any place on the field that defenses could never stop worrying about him. He certainly made my job easier.

We became close friends and kidded each other incessantly. One day I was holding a dummy for him while he practiced his blocking techniques. When I wasn't looking, he threw a block on me and knocked me on my ass. I got up and chased him all over the field, finally cornering him against the fence. I was about to grab him when he put a move on me, those feet going into that little dance of his, and I missed him, turning my ankle on the sprinkler. I lay on the ground, laughing so hard I could hardly move, and when I looked up, there was Coach Landry staring down at me, a humorless expression on his face. Needless to say, I got up without a limp.

One old problem remained: I just had to get out of camp every now and then to get away from football for a couple of hours. One night, in training camp, I tried the old ruse of propping a coat hanger and pillows under my blanket, fashioning a perfect mock-up of a sleeping body. I even had a blond wig to lay on the pillow. I was putting the finishing touches on this masterpiece when I heard a soft chuckle behind me. I turned, and there was Dick Nolan, Landry's top assistant, with his ever-ready clipboard.

"Going somewhere?" he asked.

I gave him my most innocent look, hoping to salvage the fifty dollars it would cost me.

"Why, Coach, whatever gave you *that* idea?"

There was no doubt about it, I still devoted myself to enjoyment, and I suppose I was as good at that as any man could possibly be. The way I figured it, what's wrong with that? I wasn't hurting anyone, was I?

Yes, I was. It added up to nothing. I was playing a game, both on and off the field, and I didn't even know it. I was fighting for my right to enjoy life as if it were my main reason for existence. And everyone was approving it, everyone was making it glorious . . . or so it seemed.

A serious thought seldom passed through my head, and when it did, it would be immediately repressed. I avoided any serious involvements with women. There was simply no room for that sort of thing because I didn't want any responsibilities or obligations. The same thing with books. Although I was relatively well read, I had developed a built-in warning system that made serious reading somewhat alien to my life-style. On a plane trip once, I asked Pete if I could borrow his copy of *The Rubaiyat*. I'd heard about the book and wanted to see if I'd like it. I read about ten pages and then decided to go to the lounge to check out the stewardesses.

I still hadn't grown up.

My life seemed to be full of humorous incidents, memorable for their zaniness. Like the time I was awakened at 6 A.M. by a girl who'd stayed over at my place. She had to go to work; would I please get up and take her home? So naturally I would, half-asleep, in my underwear, too stupid and too groggy to bother putting pants on. The garage was attached to the apartment. I thought I'd just drive her home, put the car back in the garage, and get back in bed; who would see me at that hour?

I didn't know I'd run out of gas on the way home.

That woke me up, all right. I was out on the main highway, at least three blocks from the nearest gas station. I must have sat there for thirty minutes trying to figure out how to handle this. Time was working against me, since traffic was beginning to build up. Finally I realized I'd have to take the bull by the horns and walk to the station. Since I was practically nude, I decided to run. I hid behind a gas pump while the attendant was cleaning somebody's windshield. When he came close enough, I signaled him: "Pssst!"

He didn't hear me, but another car pulled in behind me, so there was no way I could continue to hide.

I stood up and faced the music.

The guy looked at me and couldn't believe what he saw. He just couldn't believe it!

"Look, buddy . . . I ran out of gas back there. . . ."

He didn't say a word. He just kept staring at me, starting to smile a little bit. I knew I had to move quickly because I didn't want to be recognized. And I obviously couldn't tell anyone who I was.

"Listen, I *really* need some gas."

"You got any money?"

"No. How could I have any money?"

"Sorry, mister. No money, no gas. I can't give it away."

"Look, I'll pay you later."

"How do I know that? It'll be my ass. The gas can alone is worth a couple of bucks."

"I swear—"

142

"You know something, you're really nuts!"

People were laughing like hell. There were three cars at the station now, and the wisecracks were coming in fast and furious. I kept hiding my face with my hand, desperately trying to avoid being recognized. I kept thinking, all I need is for someone to have a camera, then I'll really be in trouble.

"Please . . . please!"

Finally he agreed. I left with the gallon can and started the long run back to my car, too embarrassed to look back, recrossing the highway to the sound of screeching brakes and honking horns and catcalls. I made it back and started pouring the gas in, thinking, Jesus, I'm going to get away with this, nobody knew me, it's all going to end up roses.

I finished, put the cap back on, and was about to get into the car when I heard giggling from nearby. I turned around and saw a carload of people watching me.

"Hey, Lance, is that a new outfit you're wearing?"

"Styles sure are changing."

"Where'd you get that shirt, Lance?"

I acted as though I didn't hear them. I did better than that, I acted as though I weren't even there. I just got into the car and drove home. I'd pay the attendant later. I climbed into bed, pulled the covers over my head, and went back to sleep, convinced that this whole damn thing had never really happened.

The life of a growing boy.

X

The Dallas Cowboys were an inconsistent team in 1967, just good enough to win our conference, yet beating Cleveland for the Eastern title, 52–14. We were a team that provoked all kinds of comments. Some said we were great, others said quite the opposite. It all depended on which game they saw us play. To see them all was no great help; we beat good ball clubs and lost to poor ones. We did some things right one game, wrong the next. We were a team that had not yet learned its own strength, just its weaknesses.

It followed, then, that we were not entirely secure. The team had plenty of heart but not quite enough confidence. We had yet to establish our identity: a running team? a passing team? a defensive team? What kind of game were we supposed to be known for? Above all, was it a team that could win it all?

The year before, the Cowboys had won the Eastern title and had lost to Green Bay for the NFL Championship. Dallas had played admirably, especially for a young club facing such an experienced and talented team as the Packers. Yet you would hear some talk and read some newspaper stories that we were strictly in-and-outers, and that quarterback Don Meredith was a choker who could never win the big one. Though there was no justification for this viewpoint, football buffs made hay out of idle conversation and one opinion was as valid as another in this land of free speech. It was the nature of fans to speculate. It was even considered to be good for business. The trouble was that the Cowboys were sensitive—as untested teams are wont to be—and a piece of their collective mind wondered if it were indeed so. It's amazing how you can read something about yourself that you *know* is absolute nonsense, but because it is in the newspapers it has a certain impact, it gets inside of you, it leaves you vulnerable, you start thinking that you have to *prove* that it isn't so, and if you have to prove it, then maybe it *is* so.

I had been with the Cowboys for only one season, but I felt I knew them extremely well. In fact, because I'd come from the outside, it could be said that I knew them better than they knew themselves. I felt that we were definitely the team of the future, the best team in football. We had tremendous speed, an offense famed for making the big play, and an exceptionally strong defense. Tom Landry was a brilliant coach with a fantastic football mind and a rare capacity for organization. The Cowboy front office was on top of everything. Tex Schramm was a tough but excellent general manager, one of the prime moving forces in professional football. Clint Murchison, the owner, was just that; he never interfered. The entire staff, right down the line, was as good as anyone could find. Every player knew this and respected it. It was definitely the sort of thing that mattered. All this club needed was to complete that final hurdle, the NFL Championship, the *proof* of our talents.

This was the Dallas Cowboys as we flew up to Wisconsin to play Green Bay for the 1967 NFL title.

I will never forget anything about that game. Its impact was so great, it had a permanent effect on all of us. It was very cold, fifteen degrees, when we arrived on Friday, December 29, two days before the game. We boarded a bus and headed for Appleton, Wisconsin, our headquarters during our stay. We spent the next hour touring the town, the mayor's welcoming idea, I guess, but there wasn't anything interesting to see in Appleton.

On Saturday we worked out on Lambeau Field, the late Vince Lombardi's monument to football, a grass surface with a few hundred thousand dollars' worth of heating pipes a foot below the ground to prevent it from becoming frozen. They called it the biggest electric blanket in the world. Considering the weather, the field was in great shape, frozen only in spots. We were a lightning-fast team depending largely on speed and finesse. Our offense utilized multiple formations with quick-striking runs and long passes, and our defense was based on discipline and coordination between its individual members. It's understandable, therefore, why the playing conditions were so important to us. We had hoped for warmer temperatures, but there was no wind, and the footing was good, so, all in all, we were very pleased.

On Sunday morning, the day of the game, the phone rang in our hotel room, waking my roommate, Ralph Neely, and me.

"Good morning," chirped the operator. "It's 8 A.M., it's fifteen degrees below zero, and the wind is twenty miles per hour, from the north. . . ."

I gasped, rubbed my eyes, and looked out the window.

Or, more accurately, I looked *at* the window. The glass was so iced up, I could not see through it.

"Holy shit!" I gasped.

"What's the matter?" asked Ralph.

"Siberia," I said.

Neely mumbled something about pass receivers being too delicate. Then he got up to go to the can, and when he came out, he made his own comment.

"Holy shit!" he said.

The temperature had dropped thirty degrees. By the end of the game, it would drop ten degrees more. And to make matters worse, we now had a strong wind to contend with.

We went downstairs to our pre-game meal, and everybody was pretty depressed. Some of the players started making jokes about it, because they didn't know what else to do. Others began to complain.

"All right, all right," Landry said calmly. "It's the same temperature for them, too."

It wasn't the same, though, and everybody knew it. It nullified our one big advantage over the Packers: speed.

In the locker room, we did everything we could: we wrapped our feet in Saran Wrap and covered them with socks and prayers. We also put on thermal underwear. And there were a few more jokes, but nobody laughed anymore.

We came out on the field for the warm-ups, and the surface was pure ice. It was as if the plug on the heating system had been pulled. It was frozen solid. A marble floor was softer. And, of course, there was absolutely no footing.

It was so cold, I could hardly breathe. It was crazy. How could anyone play football in this weather? I didn't want to play. Nobody wanted to play. It should be postponed, I thought. It's not fair to either team. I watched one of the trumpet players in the band try to play his instrument, and

147

his lips froze to the mouthpiece. They canceled the half-time show, but they didn't cancel the game.

We started badly. In the first half Bart Starr threw the ball like a man with warm hands, and Boyd Dowler caught two touchdown passes before we even got close to their goal line. We were in trouble; Meredith was working hard but couldn't cope with the cold. He was throwing poorly. His face was so frozen, he could barely call the plays in the huddle. What we hated most was leaving the canvas tents on the sidelines, where infrared heaters blew in warm air, only to come on the field and hear the ref call an official time-out for a television commercial. You'd have to stand there for a solid sixty seconds, and by the end of them your hands were numb. I never understood why they didn't let us wait in those tents.

Then we got lucky. Starr tried to pass, but his receivers were covered, and Willie Townes hit Starr, causing him to fumble. George Andrie, already with seriously frostbitten toes, picked up the loose ball and ran it over for a touch-down: 14-7. A few minutes later, Willie Wood fumbled a fair catch, and we recovered at the seventeen; Danny Villanueva kicked a field goal, and we went into the locker room only four points down at half time.

We were still alive. It was still anybody's ball game. You could feel the anger and the frustration in the locker room and, above all, a tremendous determination to pull this one out. Guys were hollering, "Fuck the cold, let's go get 'em!" There were no jokes this time. Not even a smile. I'd never seen Meredith so intense. Landry was great: very solid, all business. The icicles had been hanging from his nose out there, but his mind never stopped working. He recommended certain changes in blocking assignments, because of the field conditions. He told us we could move the ball on the ground, if we'd keep hitting the way we did in the second quarter. He said he saw no reason why we couldn't win it, even if we didn't get any more breaks, even if they got them. He sent us out for the second half with a positive feeling.

Still, it was up to Meredith. He had hit only four out of thirteen passes in the first half, and one interception. Statistics like that don't help the running game either. The big question was, could Don move the club in the second half?

He did. He had cut a hole in his jersey and kept his hand warm against his stomach, and we pushed them all over the field. In the first series, we took the ball from our own eleven all the way down to Green Bay's thirteen, then Don scrambled for nine more, but he fumbled and we lost possession.

We held them and took over again. I caught my first pass on the next series, hit that hard ground and didn't think I'd be able to get up. I'd never felt anything like it! My back hurt me for the rest of the game.

All during the third quarter, I kept watching their strong safety when we'd pitch out to Danny Reeves on the sweep. Reeves was making good yardage in the second half and it bothered them, I could see that. Both Willie Wood and Bob Jeter were becoming very sensitive about shutting him off. All season long, Reeves had been successful with this play, and because of it we were even more successful with the option pass that he threw so well.

As the last quarter started, I told Meredith: this is what we've been waiting for. They're playing the run. Let's throw the option.

Meredith called it.

He called the play to the left side. Since it was more difficult to throw to that side, they would be less likely to expect a pass. I came off the line simulating a run, trying to make Wood think I was going to block him. I got down low and made my move right into him. As Reeves came around the end, Wood slid off my fake block, and out of the corner of my eye I saw Jeter move up to shut off the sweep. Immediately I straightened up and took off downfield.

I knew right then that I had both of them beaten hopelessly. It was going to be a touchdown, I really knew it, and it was the most marvelous goddamn feeling in the world. I looked back over my shoulder for the ball, and I realized that it was a little too short, I had to slow down, no, I had to stop! And suddenly I thought, shit, I'm going to slip on the ice. I could feel my feet sliding out from under me, the ball was changing directions in the wind; it had turned from the best to the worst feeling I ever had. But I kept my balance by catching the ball standing still. I saw Tom Brown coming for me, and I took off for the corner about forty yards away, praying for footing as I cut loose. When I crossed that goal line, I was suddenly very warm.

We were ahead for the first time, 17–14.

For the rest of the period, it was just a question of keeping the ball as much as possible, so we could run out the clock. With about two minutes left, we were forced to punt, but they had over seventy yards to go for a touchdown. Time was running out. This was obviously their last series. If they lost possession this time, there was no way they could win.

On the first play, Willie Townes broke through and tossed Starr for a nine-yard loss. I stood on the sidelines with that fantastic feeling that accompanies anticipated victory when you don't really believe it, it's too good to be true.

It was. On the next play, they started their incredible drive. Starr threw two flat passes to Donny Anderson and they made the first down. The next thing I knew, they were on our thirty with a minute to go. This time Starr threw to Chuck Mercein, who was tackled on our eleven. I didn't know what to think. I couldn't believe we'd lose. I thought, hell, they'd go for a field goal and send the game into a sudden-death overtime. Then Starr called a great play. Most teams normally pull both guards to lead the blocking on end sweeps. But Bob Lilly is so quick that he will break into the backfield behind the pulling guard and catch the running back before he can get back to the line of scrimmage. On this play, however, they suckered him into chasing the wrong back. They sent Mercein through on a cross buck in the area Lilly had vacated, and Mercein made his way to the one. I stood there, motionless. I couldn't speak, I couldn't holler. I could only feel an impending sense of doom. Twice Starr sent Anderson at the line, and both times we stopped him. He took his last time-out and went over to talk with Lombardi. What the hell were they going to do on third down with sixteen seconds left? Send Anderson on a sweep, with the option to pass or run? A play action pass, so if it's incomplete, the clock stops, and they can have time to attempt the tying field goal? All I could do was guess.

"I couldn't get a footing," Bob Lilly said later. "I wanted to call time to get something to dig me a foothold. . . ."

As they left the huddle, I had decided they were going to pass. Nothing else made sense. If they ran and didn't make a touchdown, then time would run out before their field goal team could line up, and they'd lose. I begged him to pass, to throw it away. Let them kick the field goal. We'd get them in sudden death.

Then, behind a great block by Jerry Kramer, Starr carried it over on a quarterback sneak, a totally unexpected play. Everything fell out of me, the whole works. I knew that something terribly important had happened, that I'd never be the same, and neither would the Cowboys. There was something very weird about that feeling. Every club loses games, little ones, big ones. Nobody wins them all. But this was different. It was so cold, we'd been behind by two touchdowns and we'd come back, we didn't give up, we'd put out more effort than we ever had before. We didn't deserve to lose. It didn't make a damn bit of sense.

We got the ball again after the kickoff. There were still a few seconds left. Don called for Hayes and me to run a streak pattern, even though they would definitely be expecting it, but we had to try it. I lined up thinking that he would be looking for Bob first, and as I approached Herb Adderley, I hesitated for an instant, cutting my stride ever so slightly. I wasn't loafing, but I didn't really drive by him the way I could have, because I already had him beaten. Then I looked back and saw that Don had thrown it to me, not Hayes. The ball was a yard beyond my reach. I had cost myself at least a couple of feet all because I'd broken stride, all because I hadn't fully concentrated. I might have caught that ball, and if I had, I probably would have gone the whole way. I'll never know if anyone else was close enough to catch me, there was still fifty yards to the goal, but I had Adderley beat. I could have won that game on the last play.

I have berated myself ever since for that failure. I can still see that ball in my mind's eye, I can still feel myself reaching for it. . . .

The locker room was a tomb. Some were crying, others sat there bleeding inside. I saw guys smashing their lockers with their fists. Everybody in that room had left something out on that field. Everybody knew that this would be a winter during which we'd play that game over and over in our minds, trying to understand why we failed, and not being able to come up with an answer.

And Don, poor Don. He took it all on himself. He told

152

the press he'd played very badly and that was the difference between the two clubs. Nonsense. The press responded by saying that Meredith would never win the big ones, that he couldn't come through in the clutch. Also nonsense. The Dallas Cowboys lost, not Don Meredith.

The press turned on us that day. We became known as the team that couldn't win the big ones, the team that had no character. We read it in the papers repeatedly over that long winter, we heard it on TV, we faced it in the streets, in restaurants, at parties. Chokers. It didn't matter that we'd fought our way back, that Green Bay had a tremendous football club, that the field conditions were especially harmful to our style of play—all that mattered was that we'd been beaten. The argument was that no team with our personnel should have lost. Period.

All of this created problems, serious problems. We heard it so often, a part of us wondered if it were true, and once that set in, once that cancer started to work, the whole organization began to contend with its image. This resulted in the so-called self-fulfilling prophecy.

XI

I went to Los Angeles in January of 1968 to meet with some record producers who had shown an interest in me. I signed a contract with Columbia and cut my first (and, as it turned out, my last) record for them a few months later. Although I must admit it didn't exactly set the music world on its ear, it was certainly nothing to be ashamed of, either. It even got to be the number-two song in Keokuk, Iowa—a source of immense satisfaction to me.

I liked the L.A. area so much, I decided to live there during the off-season. Los Angeles had everything a bachelor could want: lots of places to go at night, lots of friends, parties, action. It seemed almost as if there was an entire section of America set aside for young people without families or burdensome responsibilities. I am serious when I say that one could go for days and never be conscious of seeing anyone over thirty.

It was a happy time for me. I had made it big as a football player in Dallas. It gave me confidence, plenty of money, and, perhaps above all, access to the fair sex. Of course, I wanted more than that, but my initial concern was always physical. I couldn't get interested in a girl mentally unless she was attractive to me physically. I'd had a deep feeling for Marcia through all those years, but I just didn't want to be tied down at the time. I was always looking around for something else, for something better, maybe, something that would be a new challenge. I really don't know what I was looking for. Something absolutely perfect, because you couldn't find many better than Marcia. I would go skipping around the Hollywood night-club circuit, always on the loose, looking for whatever might seem interesting. At times, though, I wondered if I wasn't overdoing it. Every so often I'd stop and ask my-self, what am I trying to prove?

Nevertheless, I enjoyed my way of life for the most part. Although I was getting to the age when I actually thought about marriage, I had mixed feelings about it, doubting that there was a woman I would want to be with on a permanent basis.

During the course of my Hollywood meandering, I spent a lot of time at The Factory, an exclusive nightclub run by a man named Ronny Buck. I was extremely impressed—it had class, and there was always something going on there. Ronny introduced me to more dollies in one night than I'd ever met in my life, and they were the type I really liked: respected, intelligent, beautiful. It got to where I was at that place almost every night.

And then came May 8, 1968, a day I'll always remember.

There's a scene in *The Godfather* where Michael Corleone is in Sicily hiding out, and all of a sudden he comes across a fascinating peasant girl, and he immediately falls in love with her. His friends tell him he has been "hit by the thunderbolt."

That's what happened to me when I first saw Joey Heatherton.

I was with a friend, George Hill, who wanted to introduce me to Bob Sidney, the choreographer for *The Dean Martin Show*. George asked me to go with him to the final taping of the summer replacement series, which Joey co-hosted. I knew who she was, of course, and I was curious to see what she was like. I met Bob just before the dress rehearsal began. His first remark to me was, "Why, my chorus girls are in better shape than you are!" I liked him right away, I liked that open kind of put-down, but it was nothing compared to what followed. Joey came up to Bob to ask him a question about one of her numbers, and he introduced me to her.

"Hi," she said.

I looked at her, and yes, that thunderbolt had hit me. She stood there with her hands on her hips in black leotards, and she had the most stunning figure I'd ever seen. I expected to see a good-looker, but she was infinitely more than that. Long blond hair, clear skin, no makeup, a natural loveliness. She was too much.

She smiled at me, but her mind was on her work. She was thinking about a dance step she had to do on stage in a moment, and she soon excused herself. I immediately sensed that she was a perfectionist, one who took great pride in her work, who wasn't satisfied until she had done something right.

I couldn't take my eyes off her after that. Later, as the show was being taped, I watched her intently. I'd never seen anyone who had affected me so. When she sang a solo ballad, I went up to the control booth, where there were a half dozen monitor screens, and the room was full of her sound, full of feeling and style. It completely floored me. I didn't know how talented she was. Apparently the others reacted in the same way.

I was invited to the cast party, a traditional affair after the last show. I went, but I didn't know that many people to talk to. I just stood in the corner and kept my eye on Joey as she moved around the room talking to everyone. They all seemed to like her as a person. Finally she ended up where I was, and again she said, "Hi."

"I know it must sound sort of stupid to say this, but I was amazed at the way you sang. I mean, it got to me."

"Well, thanks," she said.

"I thought the show was excellent."

"Oh, was it?"

"And you were terrific."

"Well, thanks a lot. . . ."

"I really mean it."

She smiled, and I stopped with this drivel. I was thinking what typical show-biz talk I was throwing at her, but I couldn't help myself, I was telling her the truth. But I was afraid that it was sounding kind of phony.

"Look, Joey, I know I have no right to ask you this, but after the party, I wonder if you'd like to come over with me to The Factory, if you're not doing anything special. . . ."

She'd refuse, I figured. I was handling all of this badly. A girl like Joey has got to expect better lines than those I'd opened with.

"That would be nice," she said.

She had her friend with her, a lovely girl named Dale Weiland, who was a sort of personal secretary and companion. She and Bob Sidney went along with us. We sat at a table in the back, and I began to ask Joey questions about herself. Not the usual questions, but what was she really like, what did she think about? I wanted to get to know her.

I could see that Joey was essentially a shy, unpretentious person, with an air of mystery about her. And that made

157

me want to know her even more. She didn't like to talk about herself, preferring to talk about me. She told me that Frank Sinatra, Jr., who had been the co-host on the show with her, had pointed me out, identifying me as the one who almost won the Green Bay game. He gave me the big buildup, but this didn't mean that much to her, since she didn't watch football that often. Actually, I liked that. I wanted to be taken for myself.

By the end of the evening, I was asking myself if it was love at first sight. I didn't know what to do about it, though, so I did nothing. As much as I wanted to see her again, I felt a little hesitant about asking her, so I didn't. I guess it was because I couldn't guess what was going on in her head—perhaps I was afraid of being turned down.

But as we started to leave, Bob Sidney invited the three of us over for dinner the next night. And I was elated. It turned out to be a great evening. I kept thinking about how completely real Joey was, no pretense of any kind. She was not even the least bit affected as many people in show business are. She did not put on airs, she said what she really meant, she was down-to-earth. She seemed to have everything I wanted in a woman—sincerity, intelligence, talent, glamour, and incredible beauty. I sat there, the second time I'd been with her, and I'm thinking, hell, she's perfect for me. She's independent, she has her own life to live, she wouldn't be the classic little housewife waiting for the hardworking husband to come home to tell him what a dandy casserole she'd cooked.

But I didn't say a word, not one word. When I took her home, I walked into the fantastic house she had rented—a swimming pool right in the center of it, with a great view—and it made my apartment look like low-rent housing. It was intimidating, almost as if it were out of my league. We sat up until early in the morning, eating ice cream and talking, and I left, not making any sort of move. I just waved good-bye.

158

I called her the next day, all ready to take her out to dinner, candlelight and wine, just the two of us. . . . Then she told me she was going back to New York that evening.

It hit hard. I didn't know what to say except to offer to give her a ride to the airport. No, she said, she had a rented car she had to return. Well, maybe I'd drop over just to say hello—and good-bye.

It was a lot easier to say hello. Neither of us said very much. She was finishing her packing, with Dale's help, and I just sat around trying to appear casual. There was only one moment of importance, but it was enough to light me up: I looked up once and saw her staring at me, and we held each other's eyes for what must have been ten or fifteen seconds, and I knew then that she was interested in me; I didn't know how much, but something was happening.

She gave me her phone number in New York, and then she left. I didn't know what was going to happen between us, it had all happened so fast. But I knew for sure that I felt something different.

There was absolutely no doubt about that.

XII

I went back to my apartment, turned on some music, and tried to make sense out of the way I felt. Since I had never felt about anyone that way before, nothing made sense. At any rate, she was gone, and I had to make the best of that. There was no point in dreaming up any campaigns, starting with tender little phone calls that very night. The thing for me to do was to be myself. Besides, I had work to do. I had made up my mind to open a club in Dallas, along the lines of The Factory—hopefully with the same taste, style, and exclusivity. I named it the Pearl Street Warehouse.

Then, too, there was the little matter of preparing myself for my chosen profession, for the season was about to begin again. And so I began running. I ran every day. I don't enjoy running: it's boring. It makes me tired, sometimes so tired that my body is crying out in pain. When that happens, my body inevitably asks my head, what in the hell are you torturing me for? But I know that my body has to learn to live with that sort of pain, and that my head has to ignore these questions. In fact, my head has to tell my body to keep right on running, and faster, too.

I ran a lot, just as I do every year about that time. Speed, quickness, and endurance are vital to my position. A wide receiver is paid to run and catch the ball. The more you run in June, the more you can catch the ball in July and August. And if you don't catch the ball in July and August, you don't get to wear a football uniform in September. Somebody else wears your uniform. And if you don't get to wear a uniform, they don't pay you any money. And that's not the way it's supposed to work out.

I therefore ran myself into the best condition possible. When I showed up at training camp in Thousand Oaks, California, I was ready to play.

I was also ready for other things, and that started costing me money. In fact, it wasn't long before I got the feeling I was financing the entire summer camp operation. It all began when the team took a chartered bus to Los Angeles to watch the Rams' first exhibition game. We were to face them two weeks later. I didn't think they would check the bus on the return trip, and I figured they'd skip bed check, since we wouldn't get back until after midnight. So I arranged a rendezvous at the Coliseum and planned to make it back to camp by breakfast. I was wrong about the bus check, and I was wrong about the bed check. I pulled in around eight in the morning and Ralph Neely gave me the bad news.

And bad news it was. For this would not be a token fine, this was the big apple: $100 per hour. I sat down on my bed and put my mind in gear. There had to be a story I could cook up for Coach Landry, something to evoke his sympathy, an excuse to end all excuses. I was going to be put to the full test this time. The way I figured it, I was about eight hours late, so I needed about $800 worth of imagination, and I needed it fast. Every minute I delayed in reporting to Landry was going to cost me almost $2 more.

Fear began to inspire me. For example:

A. I was walking to the bus after the game and I had a sudden dizzy spell (Landry knew I'd had a number of concussions in the past) and thought it best if I stopped and rested for a few minutes, but, incredibly, I fell fast asleep until 3 A.M. and had to take a cab back to camp. (Not bad, I thought: late because of injuries suffered in combat.)

B. I was going back to the bus when I saw a woman become violently ill, throwing up and all; she obviously had some sort of food poisoning. I finally got a doctor to come over, but it was so serious, I couldn't leave her. (You can't fault a man for chivalry, can you?)

C. My kid brother, Chris, came to Los Angeles after running away from home, and I had to leave the game and sit up with him all night convincing him that it was a foolish thing to do. (He had to admire my family loyalty, didn't he?)

Of course, each of these would be embellished and filled with nuances—I was master of the nuance—and delivered with just the right level of cool, never overstating, never pushing too hard. Admittedly, it was tough to work on a man like Landry, his mind was too quick, too well organized, too disciplined. Still, he was compassionate, and if I hit him with the right story in the right way at the right moment . . .

I had it narrowed down to the above three, not knowing which one I would use. I figured I would make up my mind at the last second, depending on the way the conversation seemed to be going.

I stopped by his table at breakfast, so he would know I was back.

"Good morning, Coach—"

"In my room, after breakfast," he said.

Well, that gave me a few more minutes to work on it, and suffer in fear, as it turned out. I started thinking he was really down on me, he might even trade me. I managed to eat something, not much, then casually walked out, trying to create an air of confidence. I settled on C, the story involving my brother, since it was the most plausible. I would tell him that I knew it was not an excuse, and that I was prepared to pay whatever fine he might impose, but I didn't want the coach to think I had been out all night for frivolous reasons.

"Well, Lance?"

He had a stern, unfriendly look on his face, and it frightened me. He didn't comprehend anything but total dedication to football; that's the way he was as a coach, and that's the way he was as a player. His attitude and his unique intelligence made him an all-pro cornerback, even though he had limited physical ability. He just couldn't understand any fooling around, on or off the field. All this flashed through my head at that moment. How could I convince someone who didn't speak the same language? But, more importantly, how could I lie to a man I respected so much?

"Coach," I said, "I have no excuse."

He looked at me in amazement. He was prepared for a wild story, like the one I had planned to tell him. But when he realized I had nothing else to say, he took out his pen and a piece of paper and figured out the simple arithmetic of the fine.

"I guess that'll be $850."

I nodded, determined to remain silent, to stick to my principles.

"The next bus goes to the airport," he said, referring to the next game. "See if you can make that one."

"Yes, sir."

Naturally, the word got out. Everybody kidded me, and above all, they wanted to know who was worth *that* kind of money. But I kept her identity secret. She came to Dallas a couple of months later, during the season, and I took her to a team party. Dan Reeves said, "Hey, there she is, that's got to be the one!"

And, of course, the press made a big thing out of it. A reporter for the *Los Angeles Times* wrote, "There goes Rentzel again, proving that he really has the ability to make the big play!"

In August we played the Bears at Canton, Ohio, and I found out on our arrival that Joey was playing in summer stock in Warren, Ohio. I had thought about her often in the last three months, and I wanted to see her again. I called her that night and she seemed happy to hear from me, especially since I was so near. She was having a party that night, why didn't I come over for it?

I thought, maybe I could get a car and drive over there. It was only 150 miles and I didn't have to play football until the next afternoon.

"Fly to her!" said my quickly beating heart.

"Don't be an ass!" said my powers of reason.

"Don't be an ass!" repeated Ralph Neely.

"The night before a game," I mumbled. "Do you think I'm *that* crazy? . . ."

"I wouldn't let you out the door," he replied.

Raymond Berry, a great pass receiver from the Baltimore Colts, came to the Cowboys that year as an assistant coach, and he was a tremendous help. His dedication was so complete, it even rubbed off on me. He had an amazing feel for every aspect of football. The first time he showed up at practice, he had a puzzled look on his face before ten minutes had gone by. We asked him what was bothering him.

"I'm not sure, but I think there's something wrong with this field." Finally, at the end of practice, Raymond had it all figured out.

"I know: it's not wide enough!"

"What?" said Coach Landry. "We've used this practice field for five years now."

They got out the tape measure and checked it. It was two yards too narrow.

He taught me approaches on my routes, different ways to come off the line. He showed me how to get a corner-back off balance using moves I had never thought of before. He taught me to key a cornerback's feet and his stance, to note which foot was forward and how his weight was distributed, how he backpedaled and which way he turned, and if he tipped off the pass coverage in any way. We would watch films and decide how we could use these keys to our best advantage. For example: "Look at that cornerback, watch how he turns to the inside. He could never cover a sideline with an inside approach, because his whole body would be turned the wrong way. Make your initial approach to the inside, so he'll turn with you, then to the outside, there, on the fifth step, not the fourth. He can recover on the fourth, but not on the fifth. . . ."

Berry also taught us to use countermoves. He felt that when you were successful with a certain pass route, defenses will become very conscious of it, and eventually start to anticipate it. That was the time for a countermove: make them think you're going to run the pattern they're looking for, and then break in the opposite direction. For example: say we've completed several sideline passes, and then we notice the cornerback compensate by lining up farther to the outside, we know he's expecting the sideline again. We'll come out in the exact formation we've been calling the sideline from, which the defender will key, and the receiver will use the same approach off the line, which the cornerback will key also. But the receiver will run a post instead, and the defensive back will usually be out of position.

Raymond helped us all. He had a great feel for knowing when we'd had enough work. Many coaches tend to run their receivers too much in practice, and then their legs are dead on Sunday. Landry had a tendency to do this sometimes, but he would usually listen when Berry felt we'd run enough. We appreciated the way he stuck up for us. "Raymond's Raiders," we called ourselves.

As it turned out, I was having a better season than the one before. Once again I had everything going for me. Everything but Joey Heatherton—not that I hadn't tried, though. I called her every few weeks or so, just to keep my foot in the door. I thought about her frequently. But I wasn't getting any encouragement, just a lot of yes, no, maybe, sure, how-are-you, and that-would-be-nice sort of replies. It bothered me, and I thought perhaps I should just forget the whole thing.

> *Joey: I liked him. I guess I'm just naturally very reserved about things like that. It takes me time to get used to a man. I'm wary, I suppose. I thought about him a lot in New York. In fact, one day I was sitting in my apartment telling my drama coach about Lance—Mr. Football Player, Dale and I called him—and the doorbell rang. It was a delivery boy with a floral box, and in it was one yellow rose. The card read, "Hoping to get to know you better,*

Lance." It was a little sticky because I was going with another guy at the time, who was around a lot. And it seemed like every time Lance would call, maybe every three or four weeks, he would be there and I couldn't talk. I would answer him "yes" or "no," and he must have wondered what the matter was with me.

Actually, I was wondering what the matter was with *me*. I had never gone to this much trouble for a woman before, and yet I wasn't getting any results. I began to think that I was making a fool of myself.

But things were going better in football. We went to Minneapolis and beat the Vikings for our sixth win in a row. It was the first time I'd been there since my trade, and I was curious to see how the fans would react to me. It didn't take long to find out. I was booed during the pre-game introductions. Geography is strange, I thought: I was Prince Charming in Dallas; in Minneapolis I was Jack the Ripper.

Why didn't Joey do a play in Dallas?

Green Bay did. We were undefeated, but it didn't faze them, and they beat us again. I always learned something when I played against Green Bay. This time I learned it from Herb Adderley. He was one of the best cornerbacks in football, with outstanding physical ability, but I had done very well against him in the past. I was now to learn that Adderley was smart, too. Early in the game, he threw an elbow at me, catching me right under the chin, and it hurt. I was so mad, I lined up on the wrong side of the field on the next play so I could get a shot at him. Landry pulled me out of the game and really got on me. Adderley was *trying* to make me mad enough to lose my poise—which was exactly what had happened.

"You have to learn that this is a sign of respect," the

coach barked at me. "That elbow in your neck was because you're a threat now, just like Hayes! He gets that all the time, but he doesn't lose his poise."

It was true. He never fought back. Adderley was psyching me right out of my shoes. If he could get me mad enough to lose my concentration, then he had me right where he wanted me. Or, to put it another way, "When you lose your head, you'll end up losing your ass."

I learned that the best thing to do is ignore it. Don't say a word. Treat it as a compliment, because it means he fears you enough to have to resort to such tactics. But I also learned that sometimes you can use the same psychology in return—work him over, and make him lost *his* poise. Either way, as long as you don't allow yourself to be intimidated.

Our last regular-season game was in New York against the Giants. Hayes and I both needed 120 yards to go over the 1,000-yard mark, a coveted achievement. The year before, we missed by a total of six yards. I had a good day, and as the fourth quarter began, I received word from a coach in the press box that I had made it. I told Don to start throwing to Hayes, to get him over too. But something went wrong every time, and they kept missing each other.

Just like Joey and me. I had gotten her tickets, but she had to leave for Los Angeles at the last minute and couldn't make it.

We won our division easily and turned our thoughts toward our first play-off opponent, the Cleveland Browns. The experts were predicting an easy victory for us, but they also reminded fans that the Cowboys always seemed to lose the big ones. That frozen Green Bay game again. We lost because we folded under the pressure, not because they were a great team who beat us.

Was there anything to that? We'd beaten the Cleveland Browns four times in a row, so we had no reason to fear them, did we? No reason at all.

They whipped us, 31-20. See, everyone said, they're chokers!

Don Meredith didn't play well, but he had a lot of company. Landry took him out early in the second half when we trailed by fourteen points. He sat on the bench with his head buried between his knees, covered by his hands; I'd never seen him so depressed. I felt sorry for him because the fans in Dallas treated him so badly. (Weeks before, he had taken his wife, Cheryl, out to a restaurant after a loss, and some men at the bar recognized him and began booing. They continued to do so until Don and Cheryl left, completely embarrassed. No one in the restaurant made any attempt to quiet those men down. I'd heard him booed many times in the Cotton Bowl, our home field, but it was nothing compared to that experience, and it was nothing compared to the criticism he was about to receive.)

Don got on the plane with us at Cleveland, but suddenly decided he couldn't face going back to Dallas; he was so down, he didn't think he could handle it. He excused himself to Landry and took another plane to New York. I didn't blame him. That plane ride was the worst ever. Another season was over and we'd blown another crack at the Super Bowl. It seemed incredible, but it was so. We'd played poorly against Cleveland—just like a team that was supposed to lose. We were tense out there, unable to fire up and play with the kind of abandon that goes with confidence, because we were afraid of making a mistake. And when we did make a mistake, we couldn't forget about it. In short, we were playing not to lose instead of playing to win.

It felt as if a curse was upon us. What can anyone do when he's dominated by this ludicrous image? Maybe the

Cowboys needed a psychiatrist along with the orthopedic surgeon and trainers.

On the following Sunday, we beat the Vikings in the Playoff Bowl. Meredith played as though it meant everything, as if he had to prove something. He was tough out there, I could see it in the huddle; there was something extra in his style, though nobody outside of the huddle really cared about the game. But Don made everyone work, and we won.

What we didn't know was that this was his last game and he wanted to go out a winner, he wanted to walk off the field and tell the world it could shove the booing up its ass. He was thirty-one years old, at the height of his skills, and though he'd been broken apart by huge invading linemen, he always mended in time for the next game. He could take the physical pain, but the psychological abuse finally got to be too much for him.

Almost two years later, he would be sitting in the ABC broadcast booth, supplying the color commentary at one of our games. Craig Morton was having a difficult time, and Cowboy fans were now booing him, following up with a sudden rising chant that filled the Cotton Bowl: *"We want Meredith . . . We want Meredith. . . ."*

"Well, Don, they finally want you," said Howard Cosell. "You feel like suiting up?"

"Not for a million dollars," he replied.

I would afterward wonder about myself: would I ever begin to feel like that?

XIII

The football season was over, and I turned my thoughts toward the opening of the Pearl Street Warehouse. Things looked promising. I was getting some of the most important people in Texas to be on the board of directors. But there was a lot of work yet to be done. Ronny Buck was helping me out, and I had to fly to Los Angeles to meet with him around the middle of January.

I decided to call Joey to see if she would be out there for any reason. She told me she was going out to L.A. the following week to do a movie for television. I suggested that she leave early, before her shooting started, and we could spend a few days together.

I knew as soon as I asked her that it was my last request. If she said no, OK, that was it. It wasn't worth the effort to pursue it any further.

She said, OK, she'd be there; I was skeptical that she would really come.

But she did.

It was worth the eight months of waiting. She seemed even better than I remembered, if that was possible. She looked at me for a long moment, sort of up and down and all over, taking it all in, and it went right through me. I sensed that she liked the way I looked, too.

"Hi," she said.

Nothing else, just "Hi."

A couple of days later, I took Joey to see the Pro Bowl game at the L.A. Coliseum. It was a lousy day, damp, chilly, and I spread my raincoat across the seat. We ate hot dogs and drank Cokes, and it was an unusual feeling—I felt just like a fan. She had been to only a few games, so she knew very little about football. I explained everything that was happening, and she became fascinated. She compared it to her own world: the club owners were the producers, the coach was the director, the players were the actors, and so forth. She was quick to pick up the action, too. It was a wonderful afternoon, and for the first time in my life I could not remember anything about what happened on the field.

Later, I took her to the Pro Bowl party, where she met a lot of the players she had seen on the field, some of them with broken noses, bandaged hands, cut faces. "Why, they look like wounded soldiers!" she said.

Joey had all sorts of characteristics that intrigued me. That mysterious quality was always there, which made me never quite sure about her opinion of me. I'd dated enough actresses to know how different she was. She was the first one, for example, who never talked about her career or her work. Others wanted to go places where they'd be seen, always to be in the right company as though their lives depended on it. Joey wasn't the least bit interested in that.

She never called attention to herself, never sought publicity. I admired her for that. Jack Jones, the singer, told me a couple of years later that when they went to Vietnam with the Bob Hope Christmas tour, Joey was the only one in the group who wasn't always hustling off the plane to have her picture taken with Hope as he stepped off. She would wait in the background. He said she was the most sincere person he'd met in the business.

Her quietness, though, was difficult to penetrate. Many times when she felt she was in the company of others who knew more than she, she would sit without opening her mouth, listening, taking it all in. Actually, she didn't give herself nearly enough credit. When she said something, it was interesting and sensible. There was really nothing shallow about her.

She dominated my days in Los Angeles as football dominated them during summer training camp, only the emotion was greater and more difficult to handle. Since we were both used to getting our way, it was inevitable that a misunderstanding would get blown out of proportion. We had our first argument one night; I left in a burst of pride, telling her as I walked out the door that she couldn't even tell how much I cared for her.

And so I returned to Dallas. I called her several days later, but it was ostensibly for business, or so the mood of our talk seemed to indicate. She had promised to be one of the directors of the Pearl Street Warehouse and to attend its first board meeting in Dallas. I asked her if she was still going to come.

Joey: I really didn't know why Lance wanted me to come, because that sort of business was all very foreign to me. I was still mad at him and really didn't want to go, but I had made a promise. So I told him I'd be there. He met me at the airport and the first thing I told him was that I was definitely going back to L.A. the next morning.

He took me to the meeting, and I met all those important people sitting around a big table. Lance was the center of it all. He handled them beautifully. They all asked him a lot of questions about the club, and he convinced them that it was a worthwhile thing for them to lend their names to. I was very impressed with his confidence and his sincerity, and I started to forget about our misunderstanding.

Afterwards, he took me to dinner, then to a party in my honor at the home of a friend of his, Billy Bob Harris. I met a lot of people, all very nice. Then he took me back to the hotel room he had arranged for me: flowers, fruit, champagne; it was a very lovely suite. He sat me down and talked to me like I'd never been talked to before. I mean, he said things about me nobody ever said to me. He hit home, he understood me, all right, or seemed to. It was all very unusual. We hadn't even really kissed each other, not in the way lovers do, yet it was all very heavy. I was really rocked. What was going on here? I knew one thing: he was different. . . .

We served drinks at the meeting that afternoon and it began to hit me after a while. I'm not much of a drinking man. I seldom drink anything but beer or wine. But it was one of those tense times when you have to do something, you're not really yourself, so you let loose. When I finally talked to her I really let all my emotions out. I told her she had not been fair to me about our misunderstanding, that I cared for her a great deal and deserved to be trusted until I gave her reason not to. I believe I got through to her.

Well, she decided to stay for a few days. . . .

I showed her Dallas, I took her home for dinner to meet my family, I never let her out of my sight until late at night. Once after I went home, she called me real late, inviting me back; she couldn't sleep, she wanted to talk some more. I knew I was very much in love with her.

The time flew by, and the next thing I knew, she had to return to L.A. to finish the movie. I had to stay in Dallas to work on the nightclub. I wanted to be with her again as soon as possible, so I asked her to stop by Dallas on her way back to New York. She said she would.

I kept in touch frequently with her during the next week, until one night when she didn't answer the phone. I called the following morning. Still no answer. She was through with her shooting by then, so I figured she was on her way to Dallas. But I didn't hear from her that night either, and I didn't know what to make of it.

But life was crazy, or mine was, anyway; I found myself in New York a few days later to do a commercial for Pepsi-Cola. I knew Dale was back in town, so I called her to say hello, only to learn that Joey was in town also!

It was like being hit by a linebacker from the blind side.

I got up off the ground, as mad as hell. If Joey didn't care enough about me to let me know where she was, then I didn't want to see her anymore. I told Dale I would talk to her later and hung up. It wasn't long before Joey called.

"Hi."

Jesus, she's got to work on her openings.

"Dale said you're angry at me and that I should call you. Well, I'm calling."

"Is that all you can say? Do you think that's going to straighten things out?"

175

I very nearly hung up the phone, but I didn't. I loved her too much to do that. She explained to me what had happened, but it wasn't that important any longer. I just wanted to see her. We made a date for dinner on the following night. February 19, 1969. An important day in my life. . . .

We went to the Ginger Man, a place not far from her apartment. It had a nice cozy atmosphere, and it wasn't long before things began to happen to me, all very unpredictable. I'll never know how it happened, but it happened.

"Joey," I said. "I want to marry you."

The words came out of my mouth so easily it surprised me. I'd been afraid of committing myself to one woman all my life, yet I didn't even hesitate in asking her to be my wife. And for all practical purposes, I'd known her for only five weeks.

I studied her. She looked as if I'd just asked her if she wanted another glass of wine, that she didn't care one way or another.

"Well," I said, "will you?"

She was playing with her wine, staring at the half-filled glass. I watched her, suddenly frightened that she would say no. I had an impending sense of doom and told myself I shouldn't have put her on the spot like that. I decided to apologize and ask her to forget about it, I didn't want her to have to worry about hurting my feelings. I never got the words out.

"OK," she said.

As I told you, it was an important day.

XIV

It wasn't until I took Joey to Tiffany's a few days later that the idea of marriage became real to us. I bought her an engagement ring, and when she walked out wearing it, there was an incredible glow on her face. I'd never seen her look that happy before. It was as if all her doubts were suddenly blown away. She'd settled whatever was troubling her mind about getting married, about making this tremendous change in her life. She put on the ring and it was magic.

Although our relationship had begun in complete harmony, Joey would continue to have doubts about marriage, which would be reinforced by my own hidden psychological weaknesses, leading to problems between us.

She called her parents, telling them nothing, just asking them to have dinner with us; they came in from Long

177

Island and met us at "21." It was all very pleasant, and Joey was playing with the ring, turning it on her finger, taking it off, putting it back on, and then her parents saw it. They were stunned, which was understandable. It was only the second time her father had met me, and I had just been introduced to Mrs. Heatherton only minutes before. All of a sudden, their daughter was engaged. Later, Joey called her brother, Dick, and he was shocked at first. I could see why they were concerned. The Heathertons were a close family, and Joey was getting married to someone they didn't even know. But by the end of the evening I sensed that they liked me and felt better about the whole thing. And I think they could tell how much we were in love.

My parents, who had gotten to know Joey when she was in Dallas, were quite happy about it.

"I knew you'd marry her," my mom said. "I could tell by the way you looked at her."

The wedding was scheduled for April 12, 1969, at Saint Patrick's Cathedral on Fifth Avenue in New York. I flew up to New York about a week ahead of time, but I didn't see too much of Joey during the day. There was a lot to do, and little time to do it in.

At night it was a different story. Everyone was inviting us to parties. George Plimpton had a cocktail party for us in his very elegant apartment overlooking the East River. We had dinner and went to the theater with Neil Simon and his wife, whom I'd become friendly with the year before. We saw Josh Logan a few times. I liked these people, and I was honored that I was welcome among them. It seemed a long way from the country club in Oklahoma City.

Craig Morton, Don Meredith, and Ralph Neely came up early to give me some support. I'd take Joey home after our evenings out, then go out again with them until all

178

hours of the night. It damned near killed me. Some support.

It damned near killed Craig, too. We were at Jilly's having a few beers, and he went outside for some air. When he didn't return, I stepped out to look for him and he was leaning against the wall, barely able to stand, his face all bloody and beat up. Apparently a bunch of hoods were standing around and baited him; like a fool, he defied them, and they simply moved in and beat the hell out of him. Fortunately somebody called the cops and the hoods took off. It was the sort of thing that always seemed to happen to Craig wherever he went. I took him back to his hotel and sat up with him all night nursing his wounds.

The night before the wedding, my parents held a rehearsal dinner at the Sky Club on top of the Pan Am Building. After the food had been served, my friends went to work on me, making speeches about what a wild character I'd been. They told some real crazy stories, ones I hadn't thought about for years. When it was Craig's turn, he stood up with his bandaged face, all cut up and swollen, and everybody laughed even before he said a word.

"I don't know," he began. "Every time I get together with Lance, something like this always happens to me. . . ."

Don Meredith had written a hilarious poem about me, called "An Ode to Sir Lancelot." My brothers, Del and Chris, added fuel to the fire, all very funny, but so centered on me, I began to feel embarrassed. I could feel the unhappy imbalance of it.

I hadn't planned to say anything, but to me Joey should have been the focus of attention. When I got up to speak, I was only interested in putting everything back in perspective.

"I've heard so many stories about me, I almost want to go and hide someplace. As you guys well know, I could enlighten everyone on some of your escapades, and since I've got the last word here, I'm sorely tempted to. But I'd much rather talk about what's really on my mind. I've never met anyone like Joey, and I can't let this evening go by without saying what she means to me. Like everybody else, I've been through some difficult times, I expect I'll go through some more, but I feel as though I could make it through anything now that I have her. I never dreamed I'd find anyone like that."

My emotions were pouring out of me, and my voice began to falter. I looked up and saw that they were all very moved, they could see how much I truly loved this girl. And then everyone toasted her. I sat down, looking at her for the first time since I'd begun speaking. She had that glow on her face again.

Don and Craig woke me up the next morning.

"Well, hello there, sucker," they said. "Today's the big day."

I wasn't nervous, but the significance of it sure rocked me. They picked me up at the Plaza, and we walked over to Reuben's for a last meal. We ate some sandwiches and kidded around, and then at the end we grew silent.

"It's hard to believe," I said. "The next time I eat I'll be married!"

We walked back to the hotel and put on our tuxedos for the ceremony, and then, finally, got into the limousine that would take me to Saint Patrick's.

I was staggered by the sight: TV cameras, photographers, and thousands of people swarming around the church. I had never anticipated anything like that, and I was sorry we hadn't decided to have a quiet, private ceremony. When Joey arrived—I didn't want to violate the tradition of not seeing her before the wedding—I went inside. But the place was terribly crowded, another ceremony was still going on, and ours would have to wait.

The next thing I knew, five men came up and surrounded me.

"Sorry about this, Mr. Rentzel, but there's been a report that some guy is going to set himself on fire in protest at your wedding."

"What!" I said. "Who?"

"We don't know. It was an anonymous phone call."

Probably a Buddhist monk, I thought. What an occasion this was going to be. I wanted tranquillity, and now it was going to be a circus. A guy was going to douse himself with kerosine, fire some shots at us, then immolate himself. I could see the stampedes, the screaming, the police, the firemen, the ambulances. . . .

"Did you bring a football?" I asked Craig.

"Football! What for?"

"I don't know, maybe we could work on a few patterns while we're waiting."

"You'd drop the ball," he said.

Finally the other wedding ended, the place emptied out, and the five detectives followed me all the way in.

The ceremony began in a hush, and when I saw Joey come down that aisle, I forgot all about the immolation. It was another moment when everything else seemed totally unimportant. I stood there watching her, thinking, this is what I've always wanted in my life.

It was all over in a few minutes; Joey and I got into the limousine, still surrounded by the huge crowd, and as we drove off, we looked at each other and just broke out laughing.

The reception at "21" was super. All of our friends were there, and Joey and I were having such a good time, we didn't want to leave. They actually had to kick us out, because newlyweds aren't supposed to stay around for very long, they're supposed to get out of there after everybody has said hello and kissed the bride and wished us luck. So we went back to the Plaza, where we always stayed, ordered up some champagne to the room and agreed that it was about as wonderful a wedding day as any couple in the world ever had.

We left the next morning for a honeymoon in the Bahamas.

XV

The press called us "America's sweethearts . . . the Golden Boy married to the most dazzling girl around . . . the ideal couple. . . ." Ours was "a marriage made in heaven."

That was overdoing it, of course. After a few months had gone by, I realized that Joey and I had gotten married before we had had time to really get to know one another. I saw that she had her faults, just like me or anyone else. Our marriage was difficult at times. It was wonderful, it was awful. We thrived, we suffered. We were turbulent, we were serene. We loved, we fought, we loved again.

Nevertheless, I wouldn't have traded places with anyone in the world.

When training camp began in July, we had settled in Los Angeles, and I went away to Thousand Oaks for the beginning of the annual warfare. It wasn't easy to be without her, especially at nights. She would come to camp to watch occasionally, and when she arrived, practice seemed to stop.

"What do you do," she asked, "just stand around all day?"

"Yeah, looking at you."

"I thought you football players were professionals."

"Nobody's perfect."

She was too good-looking, that was all there was to it.

Everyone was wondering what kind of effect marriage would have on me. It didn't take long for them to find out. I didn't break curfew once and was fined only $25 the whole time we were there. I got a lot more sleep, my concentration was better, and it made a difference in my performance. Tom Landry said that I was "the most outstanding player in training camp." It was attributed to Joey, naturally. The press ran stories saying that "marriage is going to make Lance Rentzel an all-pro." That was an oversimplification, of course, but there was no doubt that Joey was good for me.

I noticed a curious thing, however. Underneath it all, the newsmen were a little disappointed. Things weren't as exciting as they were before. I could tell that they were secretly hoping that I would revert to my old self, so they could have another escapade to write about.

Willie Townes came to their rescue. He had always had a weight problem, due to his love of food and his hatred of exercise. Also he had an amazing ability to rationalize, and this made things worse. When we weighed in on the first day of camp, Willie was ten pounds over, which set him back $500. He was furious, and as usual there was an excuse: it was because of the difference in altitude between Los Angeles and Dallas. He was naturally going to be heavier at sea level. He asked the coaches to send him back to Dallas and weigh him there, he'd prove he was right.

184

Instead, the coaches sent him to the fat man's table, where he was put on a semistarvation diet until he lost the ten pounds. Then, suddenly, Willie seemed to change. It became a daily ritual: he would drag himself into the dining hall, weak from hunger, take a few salt pills, and struggle pitifully up the stairs, back to his room in solitude.

Poor Willie.

The coaches were proud of his new attitude until the next weigh-in. Incredibly, he had gained five pounds! Willie couldn't understand. He had been starving himself for a week, hadn't he? Landry didn't know what to think.

This dilemma intrigued the reporters, and they set out to find an explanation. It wasn't long before one of them remembered seeing Townes coming in late at night with a couple of sacks in his arms. It didn't take long to figure out the answer from there, and the coaches were tipped off. They raided Willie's room after practice and found him lying in bed, finishing off a six-pack of beer and a couple of pizzas. He'd been sneaking in provisions at night!

Townes, true to himself as always, maintained that this didn't count. This wasn't a meal, it was just a little snack!

Landry said he saw Willie's point, and then said his "little snacks" had just cost him $250. He would also have to stay out late after every practice and run until he got down to his playing weight. And then, worst of all, they took his food away.

The news spread through the dorm in minutes, and everyone broke up laughing.

Poor Willie. . . .

There wasn't much laughing other than that, for the impact of our play-off defeats hung over everything and everyone. Tom Landry had an idea that maybe there was too much kidding around at practices, that the team was not serious or dedicated enough, causing us to fail in crucial situations. He made it clear that he wanted everything to be strictly business, that if everyone was completely dedicated to football for the entire season, we'd win it all.

I tried to show him that I was up to it. We went hard all summer, playing every preseason game as though it were for the championship. The Houston game in the Astrodome is a good example. The Oilers were a rough, rugged bunch with a reputation for viciousness. Fists, elbows, clotheslining, the works. In the fourth quarter, I ran a turn-in and went up for the ball, and the cornerback hit me low, upending me, and I landed on my head on that hard artificial surface. Everyone thought I had broken my neck. Somehow, I held onto the ball, but I lay there as if I were dead. The trainers revived me and started to help me off the field. I said that I didn't need any help, and I started running to the bench just to prove I wasn't really hurt. But my legs started to give out under me, so I ran faster, thinking that would keep me erect, but I couldn't, I just fell to the ground, face first, right in front of the bench. They laughed in the stands, but I had a concussion. I felt all right a few minutes later, so I asked Landry to put me back in. I caught a long pass for a touchdown on the first play, then on the next series I got upended again. I landed on my head once more, and this time I was out cold for five minutes.

After the game, my head ached so much that I felt like dying. On the plane back to Dallas, I threw up several times. It was one of those times when I asked myself why I played football. It was idiotic. I had gone back in that lousy exhibition game just to show Landry that I could be as tough as anyone. Hell, he already knew that!

Nevertheless, it was by far my best preseason ever: I scored over a touchdown a game and averaged almost twenty-six yards a catch. Then Bob Hayes got hurt right before the league opener. It put a tremendous amount of pressure on me, it seemed as if the whole secondary was working me over. It got to where I couldn't run a pass route without getting an elbow for good luck. And when I caught the ball, everybody made sure they got their licks in.

This was most evident when we played our second game at New Orleans. That stadium is a madhouse, like Fifth Avenue at rush hour; you can't hear anything, the crowd makes so much noise. The fans intimidate everyone, including the referees. The New Orleans defense had a special way of working on the opposition: they'd single out just one offensive player and combine to beat the living shit out of him. As we lined up for the first play, their safety spelled it out for me: "Rentzel, we're gonna knock your ass off."

And they did. On every play. I told that safety that it was an honor to get all of that attention, but I'd just as soon not deprive my teammates of what was rightfully theirs. I thought he would laugh. Instead he told me to go fuck myself. So I played it their way. They weren't putting much emphasis on stopping our running game, so we ran Calvin Hill on sweeps most of the time, and he had a tremendous day. Although I only caught two passes, I felt great, because I did a good job blocking and took their punishment without losing my poise. And I dealt out a little punishment when the opportunity presented itself—which meant when someone wasn't looking.

The next time we played them, Calvin Hill was their target, and they left me alone. I enjoyed that much more.

Joey had difficulty adjusting to Dallas, and I could see why. Dallas wasn't Los Angeles or New York, and there was nothing for her to do all day. She didn't know anybody, she had no function to perform, no work to do. She would go to Neiman-Marcus and shop sometimes, but she usually stayed at home and waited for me.

I thought I could help the situation by taking her to one of the first team parties to meet some of the other football wives. They felt a little ill at ease, because they didn't know if they would have anything in common with Joey, and they were understandably nervous as to how to break the ice. One of the wives decided comedy was the answer, the best way to break down the barriers. But I questioned her sense of humor. She came up to Joey, introduced herself, and said, "Saw you two on *The Mike Douglas Show.* I thought Lance was really terrific, but you were awful."

Joey thought she was very funny.

We didn't go to any more parties.

It was a bad time for us. Joey felt stagnant, and I couldn't blame her. But I didn't have any idea what to do. She came to feel that she had made a mistake in coming to Dallas with me. Naturally this caused problems, and her doubts about marriage got stronger. It bothered me a lot, and I felt quite helpless to find a solution. So I subconsciously avoided the issue as much as possible. This was a weakness on my part, and it only made things worse. I should have been more considerate of her, even though I was not to blame for the unfortunate circumstances.

However, there was no lack of love, and even when things got rough, I never once regretted marrying her. She was lovely to be with when she wasn't upset—quiet, restrained, shy in the company of others, but a great deal of fun at home alone. She simply didn't feel free in front of others unless she knew them well. Nobody knew how really funny she was. She would be watching television and then start doing wild imitations of the people on the screen. Or she would amaze me with a perfect impression of somebody we'd met before, even though he had no obvious physical characteristics or mannerisms. She simply had a fantastic ability to mimic, and she made me laugh constantly.

There were a lot of marvelous tender moments. She stirred up a tremendous emotion inside of me, and I don't see how I could ever care more for anyone.

She came to the games and got really excited by them. She could pick up very fast, she got to know football very quickly. I liked it when she was at the games, and I usually played better knowing she was there.

Craig was having a sensational season at quarterback, far and away the leading passer in the NFL, hitting 71 percent of his passes. Then, in our fourth game, he got hit by Claude Humphrey and hurt his shoulder badly. He couldn't throw all week in practice. On Sunday, against the Eagles, Craig said he thought he could play and Landry let him start. He passed for five touchdowns in the first half, and we murdered them.

"No practice for anybody this week!" was the locker-room cry.

But it was a serious injury, and he started to fade. He went through too many weeks without throwing the ball, and by the end of the season he was in terrible shape. The fans booed him, and his confidence vanished. He was a quarterback with a cannon for an arm, and now it couldn't fire. The fans never knew how much he was hurting. They began calling him "Son of Meredith."

There was a viciousness to the fans that could really crush you. We were 6–1, the best record in our conference, but when we lost to Cleveland again, everybody jumped all over us. I had been named Player of the Month in Dallas and had to go to the Cowboys' luncheon the day after the

189

game. I was making up a drill in the Air Guard and didn't have time to change clothes. The fans flocked to those things, especially when they could ask snide questions with Landry as the target.

"What did you tell the club that inspired them so much at half time?" (We'd lost 42–10.)

"How long will it take to get Don Meredith back from Africa?"

"I thought most of the Cowboys would join the Foreign Legion after Sunday's game, but I see that Lance has joined the Air Force...."

When I got up, I told them to relax. "Gentlemen, you're safe," I said. "The Air Guard will protect you. There hasn't been one enemy plane over Dallas today."

They laughed at that and got off Landry's back.

We went on to win our division championship again. Our last game was against Washington; we didn't need the victory, but I needed only fifty-eight yards to make a second thousand-yard season. I had been very busy all week, making final preparations for the grand opening of the Pearl Street Warehouse, which took place on the Friday night before the game, eight months late. The decor was even better than I'd hoped. Everything was in the style of a warehouse—crates, copper tabletops, barrel-shaped menus, Gay Nineties billiard room, stained-glass ceilings. We were mobbed. Ike and Tina Turner were the star performers, and it was a huge success.

The trouble was, I was so tied up in it that my concentration had not been on football all week. We didn't need the victory, and I figured I could easily make the yardage. But nothing was easy for me that Sunday. I dropped two passes from Craig that were right in my hands, one an easy touchdown. I ended up with only one reception, worth eighteen yards. Moral: nightclub entrepreneurs seldom break records on the gridiron.

However, it was my best season of all. I scored more

touchdowns, thirteen, than anyone else in the NFL, and my 22.4-yard average catch was tops. I made All-Pro.

Then, the play-offs again. Cleveland at Dallas. The scene was repeating itself, year after year. This time it was a rainy, cold, muddy December day. We were all fired up to play. The locker room was sharp with enthusiastic voices, the excitement was there, the place was jumping, we kept telling ourselves that there was no way the Browns could beat us.

Almost.

We started the game off well by forcing them to punt after three downs. The crowd was going wild, and so were the Cowboys, anxious to avenge two bitter losses in a row. But the ball hit one of our players, and Cleveland recovered. Almost in perfect unison, everybody's head dropped. I knew then that our confidence was already gone, it had taken only one mistake to lose it.

I turned to Hayes. "We're beaten," I said.

The Browns scored immediately, and that was it. To the most massive booing I'd ever heard, they destroyed us, 38–14. It was a miserable, humiliating day.

Four years in a row we had failed to win. The headlines in the paper the next day said it all: "OH SWELL! ANOTHER DALLAS BOOBY PRIZE!!!"

The 1969 year that had begun so promisingly ended in a dismal decline. The Pearl Street Warehouse, so promising at its inception, could not survive on the exclusive, private-club basis that was its purpose. As so often happens, the club went over its projected cost; in our case by $25,000. Although we were turning away over two hundred people a night for not having memberships, my partners began to get afraid. We needed cash for everyday operating costs, and they couldn't borrow any more money. They reluctantly decided that the only answer was to let people in without memberships.

So it was only a matter of time until our exclusive image

191

would be gone. I had an obligation to our directors, and I advised them to resign from the board. And a couple of months later, I got out also.

A year and a half of effort wasted. It left a bad taste in my mouth. The club ended up making money, but it wasn't what I wanted and expected it to be—something I could be proud of, something with real class. I did learn some valuable lessons; I didn't lose any money, but there was no sense of triumph.

As I said before, the year didn't end up an overwhelming success.

XVI

In the early part of 1970, I began thinking of more serious matters.

It was a switch, and yet it wasn't a switch. I always had an underlying desire to make a contribution to the welfare of others. I knew that there was nothing in my recent experiences that could convince anyone of that, but for all the levity in my style, I felt a tremendous need to realign my direction. Perhaps it was pretentious of me to think I could accomplish anything, but I felt strongly about doing something beyond football and selfish pleasures. I wanted to redirect my thoughts and my values toward something more meaningful. At least I wanted to try.

America seemed ripe for a new way of looking at things, especially as it related to students. I sympathized with the restlessness of the young. This is a generation that is trying to find something to believe in amid a society whose traditional values have been unsettled by vast technological and moral changes. They are attempting to discover some meaning in life, by concerning themselves with the major political and social issues in this country.

This led to a year of considerable violence on the campuses, mostly in protest against the escalation of the Vietnam War, culminating at Kent State University, where four young people were killed in a confrontation with the National Guard. The way I saw it, there had to be a better way. Something had to be done to curtail violent uprisings, to give students an organization through which they could channel their frustrations and their protests in a sensible, constructive way.

I started working on this problem, talking to people in all walks of life, representing all shades of political opinion. I went to Washington and talked with congressional and governmental leaders. I went to the Pentagon and was briefed there, I spent over an hour with the vice-president, I had an extended interview with members of the attorney general's staff. Then I went to visit campuses all over the country, trying to find a way to cement student opinion in one large all-purpose organization. I eventually met John Long, president of the American Student Bar Association, and he became executive director of a new enterprise, Student Alternatives to Violence (SAV). Headed by a steering committee representing young people of varying points of view, our program was designed to bring about a coalition of youths that would open the door to greater understanding of student attitudes in the minds of the public. We planned to put together a national conference in the spring of 1971 to find a consensus of student viewpoints that would result in a definite program of recommendations to be made to the White House and the Congress.

I also managed to persuade a number of other people to

lend their names and their time to SAV. They were chosen because they had a special identification with the youth. Included among them were Dustin Hoffman, Elliott Gould, Glen Campbell, David Scott, and Charles Schulz.

It took months to put this together. I worked on it throughout the spring and summer of 1970, even after I began training camp. I became consumed by it. For the first time in my life, I was concentrating on doing something for what I considered to be the common good. I poured ten months and at least $10,000 of my money into this effort. But it was the best time and money I ever spent. I came to New York in the fall for a press conference to announce the formation of SAV. The media were there. They listened to what we had to say. They took our brochure depicting our goals and our methods of attaining them. Many of them asked questions, and I felt we gave definitive, realistic answers.

But they made little mention of us. If I had said the purpose of our organization was to blow up New York City, SAV would probably have gotten front-page publicity. I guess our objectives were too positive to be considered important news. But I couldn't help feeling disappointed at the lack of interest, because our aims were worthy and attainable.

Perhaps it didn't make any difference. It wasn't long before the time for violence had passed. Students were opting for a nonpolitical involvement. Suddenly there was tranquillity on the campuses as if a huge blanket had smothered all protest. Still, the need for SAV remained, and we began quietly to implement our programs on campuses in the San Francisco area. They had impressive results, and soon afterward an important national student organization expressed its desire to merge with SAV. Thus one of our primary objectives, bringing together student opinion into one large organization, was practically reached. But the government ended up denying our request for tax-exempt status, after delaying an answer for almost a year. We couldn't understand the reasons behind this, because we had made sure we met every requirement. Anyway, it became a moot question, because no one will donate any money unless you have a tax exemption. And so it wasn't too long before SAV withered and died.

Therefore it could be said that I'd failed to carry it off, that I'd wasted my time and energy for nearly a year. Certainly there was nothing much to show for it all, but when it was over, for all the frustration, I felt I had been on the right track.

And once again I learned some valuable lessons. I had become much more socially and politically aware, even though I became somewhat cynical about our government. I was left with the impression that it doesn't pay attention to anything unless it is in its best political interests to do so. I also became more skeptical toward the press, for many times it seems to be interested only in sensationalism. I got to be more doubtful about our political leaders, too. The majority of them seem to be more concerned with doing what will keep them in office than with doing what is right.

Joey began preparations for her nightclub debut at Caesar's Palace in Las Vegas, and I reported back to training camp to start another season. This time, things were *really* different. Football was to be practiced and played without smiles. If there was a tightening up in '69, that was a party compared to this. Full scrimmages with the first team offense against the first team defense. The whole discipline of the club was tougher; all outside activities were to be curtailed. Landry was pushing us, he wanted to create a new Spartan feeling on the club, and he enforced the most rigid program imaginable to remold us into a winner.

The way it went, no veteran was secure. Every job on the

club was open to any rookie, they all got equal shots. Everybody had to live up to his potential. In short, it wasn't enough to be better than your rival; you had to be as good as you could possibly be. Landry benched Hayes, for example; he didn't think he was putting out enough. He would make an example of any one of us, just to inspire the others.

As the season began, we'd start club meetings at 9:30 A.M., and we wouldn't get out until 4:30, thereby eliminating any chance for outside activities. If a coach saw a spark of frivolity, he'd jump all over us. No more foolishness. Period.

I accepted this discipline because I was willing to do anything to get us to the top. It left everyone with a somewhat shaky feeling, however, since each of us was always made aware that he could be replaced at any time. And this led to something I hadn't experienced in almost four years—a loss of confidence.

In the first exhibition game at L.A., I dropped the first pass thrown to me, and it really bothered me. I couldn't figure this; I'd dropped passes before, everybody does. Once I dropped the first two passes against Washington, yet I ended up with thirteen receptions for the game. But this time it got to me. The next pass came right at me and I was afraid I was going to drop it. And I did. That really scared me. Normally, when I'm the primary receiver, I *know* I'm going to get open and I *know* I'm going to catch it if it's anywhere near me. I concentrate on *how* I'm going to do it, which moves to make, which defense to expect—but never about catching the ball. Suddenly, that was all I was thinking about.

Yes, and then the third . . .

Landry took me out "Not your night, Lance," he said. "Don't worry about it."

I worried.

All week long, in practice, I thought about it, and I kept

dropping the ball. At Green Bay, the first pass came at me in the end zone, and it hit me in the neck. Now my coordination is going too, I thought. In practice the following week, I was so bad, I didn't want anyone to throw the ball to me. I was completely psyched out by then. In the Astrodome, against the Oilers, I did it again. It was a bad pass, but I usually made those kinds of catches all the time. After that, I was completely gone. Landry benched me for the Kansas City game. He had to. I was just thankful this was still preseason.

Against the Jets, Landry innovated a new offensive tactic, the flanker-in-motion, designed to hurt the bump-and-run defense. So they threw to me a lot, and I caught six passes without dropping any.

Then, on opening day against Philadelphia, I caught six more, including the winning touchdown, and I was OK again.

It was like being told you had cancer—then, after thinking you were going to die, you learn it was just a bad cold.

At that time the Cowboys made a trade that was finally to eliminate a fatal weakness in the secondary. Our losses to Green Bay and Cleveland in the play-offs had been primarily due to one thing: they picked us apart with their passing game, and this in turn destroyed the confidence of the whole team. The Cowboys' defense was excellent, except for the right cornerback spot, and it had become an Achilles' heel. Our opponents always attacked that vulnerable area. The rest of our defense would compensate for it, leaving themselves open elsewhere, which the other team then took advantage of immediately.

But now my old antagonist Herb Adderley was a Dallas Cowboy. He moved right into the lineup, and suddenly we had as good a secondary as there was in football. Our defense had no more weak spots, and this was to prove vital at the end of the season.

I was curious to see what he was like personally. I guess it was safe to say we didn't get along well at all on the field. But I liked Herb immediately, and we became the best of friends.

Adderley also brought an intangible quality that helped our squad as much as his physical presence: he knew what it was like to be a winner, and although Dallas had not reached its lowest point yet, this winning attitude would eventually become a part of every member on the team.

Bob Hayes was having a bad time, and Landry sat him on the bench and kept him there. (Not playing up to his potential.) And Craig Morton, he was literally dying. Compensating for his slowly healing shoulder, he had changed his throwing motion and hurt his elbow as a result. The poor guy sat on the bench stewing in frustration, his confidence oozing away.

We were winning ball games, but the sword seemed to be dangling over our heads. No one mentioned it, but everyone sensed it was there. Roger Staubach was the quarterback, with Landry sending in the plays. Against New York, we were in a tough, seesaw ball game, climaxed by the play of my dreams: the flanker-reverse-pass, which I had prodded Landry for years to put in the game plan. He finally did for this one, and he called the play in the fourth quarter. But when we lined up, New York was in the worst possible defense to try it against: the cornerback on my side was right up to the line of scrimmage, close enough to follow me into the backfield and tackle me on the run. Expecting a pass, they had also brought in an extra defensive back, and that meant trouble. I was hoping Roger would audible off, but he didn't, and I began the reverse hearing footsteps all the way. Hayes managed to get a step on Spider Lockhart, so I let it go, fifty-four yards into the wind, the best pass I had ever thrown in my life.

I got hit from both sides just as I released the ball. When

199

I looked up out of that mass of arms and legs, I saw Hayes dancing into the end zone. I was so happy, I got up and jumped for joy. Some say it was the first time I'd ever showed any such emotion on the field. After the game I told Craig and Roger to eat their hearts out—I was retiring as a passer, so that I would be certain of leading the team in that category at year's end.

Then, at St. Louis, this mysterious loss of confidence hit me once more. I dropped the first pass during warm-up, then proceeded to drop them all, every goddamn one of them. By game time, I was totally psyched out again. We were moving downfield in the first period and Roger threw a sideline pattern to me, but, as I expected, I dropped it. It would have put us inside their five-yard for an almost certain score, so it was doubly painful. They didn't throw to me anymore, which was just as well. We ended up losing the game, 20-7, and Hayes and I didn't catch a pass between us, the first time that had ever happened.

And then we lost to the Vikings, 54-13. This was the first tough ball club we had played, and they showed us how bad we were. They ran all over us. We went into the game very unsure of ourselves, and the effects were disastrous. For the first time since I'd known these guys, there were demonstrations of bickering, blaming each other, passing the buck. It wasn't a ball club anymore, it was a hen party.

Everything had become a problem now. Landry had changed our offensive philosophy, shifting from a wide-open passing game to the stolid conservative short-yardage approach. He wanted to emphasize defense and ball control. Our attack was to be built around a running game. Inevitably, we spent more time on running, less on passing. As a result, our confidence in our passing game, always our strong point, completely diminished. When we needed it, we couldn't rely on it.

In November, we lost to the Giants in New York, and the following week, on Monday night, in the Cotton Bowl, and on national television, we were thoroughly, brutally defeated by St. Louis, 38-0. It was as if the shaky roof had finally caved in. There appeared to be nothing left of us, just a bunch of washouts. Hell, we weren't even chokers anymore. We were losing every game now, not just the big ones. In all the years I'd played football, from YMCA ball through my six years as a pro, I'd never experienced anything like it. You could no longer face the others, the coaches, the guy who pumped your gas, even the people who loved you. You couldn't even face yourself.

The following day, Tuesday, November 17, we held a team meeting, and the rage was unbelievable. I'd never heard anything like that either. Ballplayers who never opened their mouths in a meeting stood up and roared at what had happened to us. We were like wounded lions cornered by a million fans, a vicious press, and a dozen rival football teams. It was strike-back time.

"Fuck 'em all!" guys hollered. "Fuck the press, fuck the fans, fuck everyone!"

"Let's play ball and bust some ass out there!"

"Don't let them get us down. They can go to hell!"

They went from rage to a crazy kind of rapture. The mood was one of furious indignation. They were agitated, but there was a sudden looseness to the mood. The roof had caved in, yes, but they had shoved aside the rubble and were out in the sunshine again. The tenseness would be gone. The fear of defeat gone. There was little chance of winning our conference this year, or so it was assumed. The Cowboys decided to play the remaining games for themselves. All of a sudden, they had everything to gain and nothing to lose. It had always been the other way around before.

Dallas was on its way to a miraculous comeback. They won the next seven games and ended up in the Super Bowl.

For me, however, the new spirit of the team didn't suffice to overcome a deep feeling of failure. The truth was, we had blown it again. There was only one truth that mattered, and that was defeat. I played football to win. I wanted that Super Bowl. I craved the championship. I'd done all the rest. I'd proved myself in a dozen ways. I wanted to win it all, and nothing else would satisfy me. At midnight on Tuesday I was still lying awake, staring into the dark, tormenting myself with the idea that I was a failure.

Wednesday, November 18, found me in a state of such depression that the world could hardly penetrate it. I went through the motions of football practice like a zombie.

Football . . . what was football? What possible importance could it have in the total scheme of things? Yet to me it had become all-important and now, even at football, I was a loser.

In fact, where was I not a loser? Look at the Pearl Street Warehouse. Had I succeeded in my ambition for that enterprise? Far from it. The venture into which I had drawn my friends with such infectious enthusiasm was a flop for all practical purposes; they knew it and I knew it.

And look at Student Alternatives to Violence. SAV couldn't even save itself, much less anyone else. My voyage into the world of meaningful social action had been another doomed expedition, and SAV, that vessel of high hopes, had sunk without a trace. Another loser.

Well, at least I had my marriage. Or did I? The truth was that while I loved Joey very much, somehow we never seemed to find complete peace together. We'd had a year

202

and a half of glorious highs and painful lows. I knew that I was failing to make Joey happy at times, that I was letting her down in some ways, but I didn't understand how.

I tried to call her in Las Vegas, where she was rehearsing for her opening the following night. No answer.

Wednesday evening loomed long and empty before me. I couldn't face making small talk or putting on a cheerful front with friends. Instead, I decided to go to a movie by myself. I wandered downtown and went in to see *2001: A Space Odyssey.*

That night I was more depressed than at any other time in my life. As I stared at the screen, I was suffering in some deep, inexplicable way, as though it was I who had lost my power source, I who had been doomed to drift hopelessly into outer space.

I had read an interview with Stanley Kubrick, who had made the film. He said that there was nothing out there in space, no transcendental meaning in life. Nothing but an empty evolutionary process that had no real purpose, just existence. Seeing the movie left me with a sense of vast futility, of emptiness, of desolation.

I'd been brought up to be religious, to believe in God, to trust that there was a divine purpose that created and guided humanity, even to feel that I was destined to do good and noble deeds in life. But the more I thought about it, the more I found myself questioning it. As I tried to apply religious faith to the problems of my own life, to the way I lived and the things I did, it didn't seem to make any sense at all.

I left the theater feeling completely confused and helpless. When I returned to my apartment, I checked my answering service and found that Joey had tried to reach me. I called her back immediately, but she had gone out to dinner with some friends.

Another sleepless night stretched ahead, so I took a

sleeping pill. For a brief instant I thought of taking 2001 of them.

The next morning I still felt low. Somehow I made my way through practice, but all I can remember about it is an extreme sense of fatigue. I was physically and mentally exhausted. After practice, I tried one more time to reach Joey. No luck.

It was Thursday, November 19.

As I left the field for home I sensed a weary feeling of loneliness, hopelessness, nothing to look forward to. I drove around aimlessly. . . .

After a while I found myself pulling over to the curb in front of a big house with a spacious lawn. I was only a few blocks from my apartment, but I didn't realize it. In fact, I didn't seem to know or care where I was or what I was doing, but I was drawn by the sight of a young girl playing in the front yard. All reason, all judgment, all foresight were momentarily suspended in my mind. It suddenly seemed that through that girl some vital reassurance would come to me.

I called her to the car as though to ask a question, exposed myself, and drove away.

The rest of the day passed by like a dream. But that night I slept well, as if some terrible danger that had threatened me was now gone. On Friday I was a new man. I plunged into the new "what-the-hell-spirit" of the Cowboys as we prepared to meet the Washington Redskins. When Sunday came, we no longer feared losing and we won easily. I played a good game and once again felt like a winner.

Then suddenly it was Monday morning and Officer Williams was ringing my mother's doorbell.

XVII

Overheard at Caesar's Palace: "There's Joey Heatherton. She must be going through hell."

It had been one thing for Joey to hear the awful news from me; my confession of sickness evoked her compassion. I was her husband, and she loved me. She was prepared to do anything, even offering to quit her successful nightclub engagement to be with me. But it was another thing entirely when the world began to explode around her, when Lance Rentzel suddenly became a figure of public ridicule and his wife was transformed overnight into a storm center of gossip and adverse publicity.

Joey did fly to L.A. to meet me, but her head wasn't meeting me at all, it was somewhere else. She had felt a tremendous need to talk seriously to me about our mutual plight and the turmoil that had been building up inside of her. Instead, I'd suggested an escape, a plunge into fun and games. Lance Rentzel was in the worst crisis of his life; he had dragged her in with him, and now he was running away from the problem!

When Joey got off the plane at the Los Angeles airport, she simply got on another plane to New York—at the very moment I was flying in from Dallas.

So I suffered through those three dreadful days. I could no longer avoid facing the fact that something was wrong with me. I was afraid. It was the worst fear I had ever experienced. Suddenly I didn't know what to do with myself. Emotions were building up inside of me until I thought my head would fly off. Finally, the moment came. I looked over the railing of that terrace and found myself staring down at the rocks and trees far below.

I pulled myself away from the rail and went back inside my apartment, where I fell on the bed and wept like a goddamn baby.

Joey called later and told me she was at the Warwick Hotel. For three hours, long distance, she poured out all the pain she had been experiencing. For the first time I had enough sense not to interrupt, not to defend myself, not to turn the conversation around to my way of seeing things. She told me she had left Los Angeles because I really didn't want to talk to her. Alone, and with a chance to think, she had come to see a number of our problems more clearly. She didn't like the way she felt about them, or about me, or about us.

When Joey finished, I realized for the first time how much I had hurt her, and I told her so. I also told her I was going to get myself straightened out, that I was through running away from my problems. I loved her and needed her, and she knew it. Finally she said she'd come home.

She came back to L.A., and we tried. We talked, and we began to reach each other on all levels. We were together again, we still loved each other, but it wasn't quite the way it had been before. I guess that was understandable, considering what we had both gone through. It left deep emotional scars on both of us.

In the months to come, I gradually got over the suffering I had brought upon myself. I will never get over the suffering I brought upon Joey.

On December 14, my case came before the grand jury. Whether or not I played football for the Cowboys again that season—and I desperately wanted that—depended on their verdict. If I were indicted, it would take months to resolve the case legally, and by then the season would be over. But the stakes were much bigger than that—my entire future was on the line.

My lawyer, Phil Burleson, was basing my case on the fact that I was already seeking medical help, that I had already been punished a great deal by the publicity, and that indicting me would only serve to punish me more. When I left the county courthouse, I was hopeful of returning to the Cowboys within a few days. They had won two more games since I'd been gone, and their prospects of making the play-offs were excellent. And I had to be there if they did. The grand jury was going to vote on my case in four days, and I flew back to L.A. to await their verdict.

On Friday, December 18, my Los Angeles attorney, Sid Gittler, called to tell me the news.

"Sorry, Lance; they indicted you."

The trouble was, I didn't expect it. Those are always the toughest blows to take. Then I realized how naïve I had been. The grand jury's only function was to determine whether there was enough evidence to indicate possible guilt, which of course there was. They had no power to consider anything else.

The Cowboys were making a tremendous comeback, and I couldn't be a part of it. To be a part had been my only hope during the past two weeks, and now it too was gone. It just about tore me apart. As happy as I was for my teammates, that's how miserable I felt for myself. I was part of them, yet apart from them. I grieved at that. I wanted to play, the team wanted me to play, there was no law that said I couldn't play, I was still an innocent man who had yet to stand trial, I was free on bail to live my life without any legal impositions. But I knew that my return would put far too many pressures on the team, and they had enough to worry about already. I had to accept it: my season, and possibly my career, was over.

It was going to be one hell of a Christmas.

Joey and I spent the holiday together in Los Angeles, staying close to our apartment. We tried hard to make it joyous and rewarding, but neither of us felt up to it. I had always gone home for Christmas, but Joey didn't care to go back to Dallas, and neither did I.

I watched the Cowboys on TV as they moved another step closer to the Super Bowl, feeling proud of them, yet aching with a terrible sense of deprivation. Although I realized that it was the best way to handle it, it hurt when there was absolutely no mention of my name. It was as if I had never existed, that I'd never been a part of the Dallas Cowboys. Suddenly I was just a fan, just another person watching football on television, and I had no guarantee that it wouldn't remain that way.

After Christmas, Joey went to Harrah's Hotel in Reno. A few days after her act opened, I followed. She was not really happy that I came. I realized that too late. She wanted to figure things out for herself, to be on her own for a while. It was another painful time for us.

The fact that people were talking about me in very disparaging ways didn't help, either. I had been sufficiently isolated during the previous weeks not to know the extent of the gossiping. I was sitting in the back of the room, watching Joey's act, and I overheard people at the adjacent table:

"I hear he's raped several women, but the Cowboy management got him off each time."

"She's left him finally. They sent him to a mental institution."

My life was becoming a laugh a minute. . . .

I thought, Jesus, this was only one table out of a hundred tables in one single club, and how many people were repeating how many different versions of that sort of talk? I sat there wondering what to do about it, how do you react to that, how do you cope with it? Are you supposed to ignore it, pretend you didn't hear?

When the show was over, the lights went back on, and I walked over to that table and stood over those people.

"How do you do," I said. "My name is Lance Rentzel, and I thought you should know the facts if you're going to talk about me. First of all, I have never come close to raping anyone, in spite of my psychological problems, and the Cowboys have never made any payoffs on my behalf. Secondly, I am still with my wife, as you can see. And last but not least, I have never even seen a mental institution. I am going to a psychiatrist twice a week, and I hope to straighten myself out in time. It was a pleasure to meet you. Good night."

The expression on their faces was absolutely unbelievable. They had no idea where I had come from, or how I had overheard their conversation. They must have thought

God had sent me to punish them for their sins. They were too embarrassed to leave after I walked away, and so they sat at the table for over twenty minutes to make sure they didn't see me in the casino.

We left Reno for Miami, where Joey had a week's engagement at the Diplomat Hotel. The Super Bowl happened to be at the same time, and Dallas, winning its last seven games in impressive fashion, was to meet Baltimore for the championship.

We stayed at the Palm Bay Club, one of our favorite places, and I avoided all contacts with the Cowboys. My life would be spent in waiting; there was absolutely nothing I could do until the trial, which would decide my fate. Naturally I heard rumors. A man with ears as sensitive as mine heard some beauts. Some of them supposedly came from very responsible sources, such as from inside the NFL offices of Commissioner Pete Rozelle himself—that I was to get a two-year probationary sentence from the courts and that I would be barred from professional football forever. That really jarred me. My first reaction was to rationalize. I tried to assure myself that it didn't make sense. Legally, I could have gone back and played the rest of this year, so why not next? There were several players in the NFL who had been convicted of crimes in the past, and they hadn't been suspended. But it still came down to one thing as far as I was concerned: my fate rested with Pete Rozelle.

I had seen Joey's act many times before, but on her opening night she sang a song for the first time: "It had to be you. . . ."

I stood in the back and watched and listened. Show business has a way of making everything seem larger than life. Performers can take simple emotions and blow them up until they make mincemeat out of you. If you're vulnerable—and vulnerable was my middle name these days—you can really take a bath in it.

> . . . Some others I've seen
> Might never be mean,
> Might never be cross
> Or try to be boss
> But they wouldn't do . . .
> For nobody else gave me a thrill,
> With all your faults, I love you still,
> It had to be you. . . .

At first I pretended that I was going to listen to the Super Bowl on radio, since the game was blacked out in the Miami area. Then I thought, well, I might go to a motel out of town and watch it on the tube. I was kidding myself. I had to go to the game, to be there. I sat in the grandstand with sunglasses on, trying to blend in with the crowd. No more than three hundred people recognized me, filling the entire section with furtive whispering and side-glances. But I couldn't leave, I had to see what happened.

The game itself was difficult for me to watch. I kept thinking of those old sports movies, where the guy runs into the stadium in the last quarter and wins the game. I didn't care much about being a hero, I just wanted to go into the Cowboy locker room, put on my uniform, and play. Hell, I would have been satisfied with sitting on the bench, as long as I could be with my team. But I could only sit and watch Dallas lose when Baltimore kicked a field goal with less than a minute remaining. The monkey was still on their back. . . .

I walked away, frustrated by the knowledge that I could

easily have made the difference between winning and losing. Just by being out there, I would have taken some of the pressure off the Cowboys' running game. But I wasn't. I wasn't because I had brought on my own downfall and failed an entire team. It may seem like nothing of consequence in the overall scheme of things—and I suppose it really doesn't matter that much in the long run—but a man lives his life wanting to achieve certain goals; trivial though they may be, they're important to him. As for me, I worked hard to be the best damn football player I could be, I wanted to be part of a championship team, it was a burning thing within me. After all those years, I'd brought myself to the very brink of it. Then I blew it all for something I didn't even understand.

It was not the kind of thing that made a man feel good about himself.

XVIII

There was a story floating around Dallas that D.A. Henry Wade had dropped the charges against me because it was no big thing. Too bad it was only a joke. There were hundreds of them. All over the country, the opening line of the day was often the new Rentzel joke.

Lance Rentzel has found the secret to success: plenty of exposure. . . . Rentzel will never be convicted because the evidence will not stand up in court. . . . In the fourth quarter, if the Cowboys are behind, Rentzel will go into the game and pull it out. . . . Rentzel is hoping for a hung jury. . . . Landry wanted to use Lance in the Super Bowl, but Lance couldn't get it up for the game. . . .

And limericks, I became notorious enough for limericks:

A wide receiver named Lance
Met a ten-year-old girl at a dance.
At intermission,
Without her permission
He showed her the thing in his pants.

Or:

A football player named Rentzel
Had a penis prehensile;
It made girls cry
When he opened his fly
Because it was thin as a pencil.

There was even a bumper sticker: KEEP IT IN YOUR PANTS, LANCE. There were cartoons galore. One had me in football uniform, facing the stands with my pants down. This work of high culture was stenciled and mimeographed by one of the county clerks, using the facilities of the Dallas County Courthouse, paid for by taxpayers. There were several others like it, all variations on the same theme.

One wag sent me a list of the Lance Rentzel Hit Parade, including such pop song titles as "Easy to Be Hard," "Baby Love," and "I Just Can't Get Hold of Myself."

But the top achievements of the best creative minds were those of the rumormongers. Most of the things that were said are so vicious that I don't think they're worth going into.

Then there were the hundreds of letters that kept pouring into the Cowboys' office, to my home, to the police station, to the newspapers. Pathetic letters from homosexuals, propositioning me. ("Dear Lance, I have always adored football players, but this is the first time I ever wrote one. I know we will like each other. Let me add

214

that I, too, play the organ. . . .") Vicious unsigned letters from people who claimed to be highly religious. ("Dear Tex Schramm: SHAME! I shall never again permit TV of Cowboy games into my God-fearing home. To have allowed such a beast to wear a Cowboy uniform is as disgusting as the sin of Lance Rentzel himself.") Angry letters from indignant fans. ("Dear Mr. Schramm: This man has no place in the football world. Get him thrown off the Dallas club and out of football. I have two young sons who worship football players; they must not be allowed to idolize such subhuman perverts. . . .") These letters had one thing in common—they were always unsigned and had no return address.

However, there were also supportive, compassionate, understanding letters, which were in the majority. They, too, came from people who used religious frames of reference; from young people of both sexes who asked that I be given help and not be made to be a criminal; and from business people and professionals on office stationery. They expressed support to the club and to me personally.

By and large, however, the floodgates had been opened to so much speculation, it was going to be difficult to keep the case in a sober, responsible perspective. There was no doubt but that I had brought much of this on myself. I had been thought of as a hotshot playboy. I had jolted everyone with my long hair and my style of dress. Dallas is a conservative town, to say the least, but nothing much was made of my appearance before—in fact, many people expressed approval. But now it meant that I was a pimp or a homosexual, known to hang out in wild company, associated with bizarre doings, parties that ended up with my name on the police blotter.

But I was infinitely less concerned with my image than I was frightened by the law. I had been indicted for a

215

felony: if found guilty, I could be sentenced for two to fifteen years in prison. I would lose the right to vote, to hold office, to own property.

"In this state, not too long ago, if you exposed yourself to a little girl, her daddy would just get a gun and shoot you," said Police Chief Forrest Keene. "You have gotten yourself involved in the kind of case that can bring more crying from the citizenry to get you removed from the face of the earth than if you'd killed somebody!"

The district attorney, Henry Wade, made no bones about how juries react: "When they see that girl up there on the witness stand telling them what you did to her, there won't be any probation, the odds are you'll get sent to the pen."

"It's largely the sensitivity people have toward children. When something is done to a child, the reactions are multiplied many times over," said my attorney, Phil Burleson. "There are literally hundreds of cases of indecent exposure to adult women, and they seldom get prosecuted. Most women take them for granted. Even the law respects this: the felony charge refers only to children under sixteen."

Texas law was very specific about this. It dealt with indecent exposure as a crime, not a sickness. Psychiatrists agree—and police officials concur—that the man who exposes himself does not molest little girls, he is not a rapist, he is not apt to commit violence. In Texas, however, he is nonetheless likened to a dangerous criminal.

And Paul Adams wanted to see that I was prosecuted to the fullest extent of the law. There were many indications of how strongly he felt about this. My parents had heard persistent reports about how this had become a cause for the Adamses, how the family was dedicated to protecting the good citizens of Dallas from allowing people like Lance

216

Rentzel to walk the streets. Mr. Adams was a responsible man, an attorney with a good reputation from a respectable law firm. He was also a devoted father. I would guess that any father would feel that way. I was very sorry for any harm I might have caused his daughter.

In my defense, I had been honest about my guilt. I had never denied it or forced him to prove his charge. I could have resorted to all sort of legal machinations that might have made the experience very difficult for him and embarrassing for his daughter. I had immediately indicated my remorse and sought psychiatric help. And then, because of my notoriety, I had been put through a barrage of abuse and publicity and rumors that served to damage me, threaten my career, and ruin my reputation far more than any court could. In short, long before the trial I had been thoroughly punished. In the eyes of the world, I was guilty—though there had not yet been a trial. It would seem, then, that Paul Adams would be inclined to show compassion.

Over the course of the months leading up to the trial, my friends Carl Oates and Bob Strauss went to see Paul Adams. My lawyer Phil Burleson talked to him. They tried to convince him that everything was being done to correct the wrong, that a tremendous dose of punishment had indeed been inflicted upon me, that I was being treated by a highly respected psychiatrist, that there was nothing to be served by putting me through a jury trial that was likely to put me in jail.

In fact, any such procedure might prove even more damaging to his daughter, for she would necessarily be put in the center of attention, both in the court itself and outside it. They reminded him that psychiatrists had illustrated the potential impact of such an action, describing other young girls who had been put through such an ordeal, of how the real trauma was the trial and the hoopla that followed rather than the original incident itself.

The Adams family remained adamant. Perhaps, to convince themselves that their insistence on prosecution was right, they firmly believed that I was guilty of other such incidents, some of them far worse than what had happened to their daughter. I did what I could to dispel such charges and even took a lie detector test. But it did no good. Said Carl Oates, "I got the impression that he [Paul Adams] thought he had a duty to his family, his neighborhood, and even to his country. His frame of mind was that he was a public protector and everyone ought to be grateful to him."

My mom and dad were very upset by this. The affair had really overwhelmed them. It crystallized all the problems that had always existed between the two of them and their relationship with me. They thought of me as a perfect son. All their references to me had always reflected that. To my mom, I was her baby, and she had smothered me with love and pride and never stopped talking about me to anyone. I was God's—and the Rentzels'—gift to America.

They never could see me in any other light. If I was mischievous and made trouble for my teachers, it was because those teachers failed to understand me. If I failed to catch a forward pass, it was because it was badly thrown. If I pleaded guilty in Minnesota to indecent exposure, I was really protecting somebody's wife from getting a bad reputation.

Now, however, it seemed that I had shattered that image of perfection. Though they clung desperately to what they wanted to feel was my innocence, the situation upset them terribly. They felt Paul Adams should have been sympathetic, and when he wasn't, they began to blame him for my plight. They initially refused to accept the fact that I was guilty, that there was something wrong with me. My problems affected them far more than the rest of the family, myself included. They worried constantly, and they were never able to get it out of their mind. Like any loving parents, they wanted to help me. This was particularly true of my dad. He was desperate to come to my aid because he felt he had failed me as a father.

So he concerned himself with my case, trying to take over the problem of saving me from punishment. Eventually this became a hassle to me, even though I understood his anxiety. I had an excellent lawyer, who was doing everything possible, so there wasn't any way Dad or anyone else could help out, except to let me know they supported me. Besides, I wanted to confront my failures and admit them and, if possible, finally correct them. I didn't blame my parents for my shortcomings, I blamed myself. I told my father that he hadn't failed me in any way and that I didn't want him to take over my defense—I was in good legal hands. But it was very hard for him to stay out of it, he was so worried. I guess I'll understand it better when I have children of my own.

I also had a long talk with my mom, and I tried to explain that she had always involved herself much too emotionally in my troubles, that she had continued to treat me as a child. I told her this made it very difficult for me to be at peace with her. In the past I would always worry about what she was going to do and how she was going to react. I could not afford that anymore. I wanted to be free to work this thing out myself.

She seemed to accept that, which I appreciated.

Meanwhile, I was in constant contact with my lawyers, trying to devise an approach to the coming trial, knowing that it would be almost impossible to have a fair one, since there had been so much publicity about the case. There was considerable discussion of how I ought to plead, guilty or not guilty, of what my chances might be with either alternative. There was also a great deal of rehashing my failure to deny this whole thing from the beginning, for if I had, there was every likelihood that I would never have been identified, that the girl would not have been able to pick me out of a lineup, and that the entire case against me would have been dismissed. It had all revolved around our initial decision to see if Paul Adams would drop the charges. So I didn't deny my involvement, but charges were not dropped.

Now I was about to be put on trial for it.

Yes, I was frightened of what might happen. It wasn't the fear of prison, it was all the other consequences that left me with a pretty grim view of my prospects. A guilty verdict would increase the possibility of my being banished from football. It would strain the delicate ties of my marriage. It would mark me for the rest of my life. A less optimistic mind might say that I'd probably already ruined myself in all these areas, and that two to fifteen years in jail would be only icing on the cake. I clung to what I called "my optimistic despair." Down but not out.

In a letter to District Attorney Henry Wade, Paul Adams said that he had steadfastly refused to dismiss the charges and stood ready and willing to cooperate with the DA's office in its prosecution. He indicated he would not object to my receiving probation if two conditions were met: first, that I appear in open court and plead guilty; and second, that the court would order a lengthy probation.

So it was that there was no trial, not in the classic sense of jury, witnesses, cross-examination. The agreement was reached among the complaining parties, the defendant, the lawyers, and the judge. It was the best that I could have hoped for in the circumstances.

On April 8, 1971, I appeared in a Dallas courtroom, with my attorneys, before Judge John Mead and a few hundred gaping court followers, and offered myself to the following colloquy:

> *State* vs. *Thomas Lance Rentzel.*
> State's ready, Your Honor. . . . Is your name Thomas Lance Rentzel?.
> Yes.
> You're accused in case #C7094248 K of the offense of exposing yourself to a female child under the age of sixteen years. Do you understand the offense charged against you?
> Yes.
> Are you guilty or not guilty as charged?
> Guilty.
> Were you made to plead guilty against your will in any way?
> No.

Phil Burleson then waived the reading of the indictment and my right to a jury trial and to any cross-examination of witnesses. He then asked me if I had ever been convicted of a felony in this or any state, or received a suspended or probated sentence for any offense, to which I replied, "No."

Then, finally, the judge pronounced sentence:

"After hearing the evidence and hearing your plea of guilty, I file a recommendation to the State to set your punishment to five years' probated sentence. . . . It is also

221

understood that another condition of probation is that the defendant is ordered to continue psychiatric treatment under the supervision of the court and the court shall receive reports as it deems necessary."

That was it. All I had to do now was to face the press, and then the rest of the world. I said to the press what I wanted everyone to know: "It has been a very trying situation, I'm sure you can all understand that. I want to work with my doctor until this whole problem is resolved. I promised that to myself. I want to think about what I want to do in the future. I really haven't had a chance to do that. . . ."

Question: "Lance, do you think you'll play football again?"

"I haven't talked to the Cowboys, I haven't talked with anyone. I was waiting for this thing to be over with. . . . I'm just sorry that I had to have my family and my wife, whom I love very much, suffer because of me. . . . There have been a lot of people who have supported me to the fullest. I would like to thank them very much. Especially, I want to thank my team, because they have stood by me to a man. I'll never forget that."

In answer to the big question of my status in football, Dallas Cowboys' general manager, Tex Schramm, said, "No comment."

Life was nothing more than a big question mark. In the Dallas morning *News,* sportswriter Bob St. John had kind words to say:

This has been four months of utter hell since he was first indicted. . . . I had some doubts about his survival. At that time Bob Hayes had told me: "It's going to be awful. But Lance is strong. He'll make it." . . . I have no idea what Tex Schramm and Tom Landry are thinking. . . . I think any planning that

222

might not include Rentzel continuing to play in Dallas, that it might be better for all concerned if he went elsewhere, I don't agree with. I think he can and should play in Dallas if he can stand up to it, which he can . . . he might well get a standing ovation when the team plays its first home game next season.

In the *Times Herald* Steve Perkins wrote:

For Lance to proceed with pro football will be a test of courage unlike anything ever faced by other NFL players. But the alternative is more unthinkable. As Rentzel says: "I just can't end my career like this."

My parents were very concerned. Dad would tell me later, "We'd never seen you look so dreadful. There were lines in your face, you were very thin, and you had that ashen look as if you'd been in prison for years."

A few weeks later, I was out playing touch football with my kid brother, Chris, and some of his friends, and he had things to say that were even worse.

"You were terrible. You played like an old man. Even my friends noticed it. They were almost embarrased for you. It was hard for me to accept that what you'd been through would have so much of an effect on you physically."

After the game, Chris challenged me to a race, a hundred yards or so. For the first time in his life, he beat me.

I was frightened, all right.

XIX

I had wandered through the spring of 1971 like a man without a country. I was thrust out in that limbo world where I had no real identity. Was I still a Cowboy or wasn't I? If not, was I still a professional football player? Apparently Tex Schramm and Tom Landry hadn't decided on this matter, and neither had Pete Rozelle, commissioner of the NFL.

Although many people in the news media had been kind to me, there were more than enough important members of the press who kept trying to see that I was banned. Walter Winchell, for example: "All good Americans should stop and beware of the biggest menace to the morals of the American youth: Lance Rentzel." In a later article, he said I was guilty of child molestation. I thought he was just trying to burn me in any way he could, but I came to realize that the public in general identifies exposure with homosexuality, molestation, and even rape. And Dick Young, syndicated sports columnist of the *New York Daily News,* devoted a number of columns to crucifying me: "I realize it's popular these days to be all-forgiving, but there must be some job outside of sports for him [Rentzel]. I just can't bring myself to write heroic stories about guys up on morals raps, any more than I could believe that a man convicted of spying for the Russians would be a good risk for the job of President of the United States. . . ."

I guess he figured that some girl would seduce me into exposing myself again, then blackmail me into telling our offensive game plan for next Sunday's game. . . .

It was enough to keep me nervous, especially since I had no firm ground to walk on. It felt as if practically everyone looked down on me. I was a freak, an object to be pointed at and commented on. I could walk into any public place in America and hear the comments behind my passing back: "Now there goes a real sex pervert. . . ."

What do you say when you hear such things about yourself over and over? What do you say to your wife, knowing that she has to face it on her own? How do you live in society when a civil word seems to be a special treat and not just a routine greeting?

I just couldn't prepare myself emotionally for this sort of confrontation. There was nothing in my life to equip me for being a man who hides in a corner. I had always been outgoing, always wanting the friendship of everyone. It had always bothered me when people didn't like me. What then when they slandered me?

Poor Joey. She would put on a brave face and pretend that it was nothing, that those who spoke such nonsense were only capable of nonsense. But it hurt. She was an entertainer, and her career depended on the public. Joey was now a hot potato. There is no doubt that her career suffered because of her association with me. She had a television special canceled. For months, every nightclub reviewer spent more space on the latest in the Lance Rentzel saga than he did on Joey's act. Some of the press were especially cruel. *Women's Wear Daily* asked for an interview while Joey was in Miami. She said she would give it if they promised that my trouble wouldn't be mentioned. The reporter agreed, saying they only wanted to do a fashion story about her. When the story appeared, Joey was not referred to by name; they called her "Mrs. Lance Rentzel" and spent two-thirds of the article on my case, ending up by informing their readers that I would be suspended from the NFL, and that my only hope was to play in Canada.

More than anything else, I wondered if I would be permitted to play football again, and if so, where. People like Frank Gifford told me I should stay in Dallas, that I should see it through, take anything the fans would dish out to me, show the town that I was stronger than all of its abuse. Even assuming that I could handle that, what effect would it have on my teammates? Wouldn't it put an unfair burden on them? Wasn't this the real reason that I dropped out at the end of the last season? Wasn't this also the reason that absolutely no mention was ever made of me over the television broadcasts of the play-off games?

If not Dallas, where then? Obviously, the most likely cities were New York and Los Angeles, the largest and most sophisticated and surely the most liberal, and places where I had a lot of friends.

In April I talked with Pete Rozelle, and he was encouraging. He said he would have a decision in two weeks. I respect him and believed he'd be fair. I also spoke with Alan Miller, former attorney for the NFL Players Association. He was frank and realistic.

"There are some guys playing the NFL who've done worse things than you. I've heard of guys doing all sorts of weird things, like taking their pants down and walking bare-ass into laundromats, others putting their rear ends out of windows and shitting all over automobiles. I've heard of guys doing things to women in public bars that you wouldn't believe. Your case has attracted a lot of attention because you're married to a glamorous star and it involved a ten-year-old girl. That's a dangerous matter for Pete Rozelle to consider. He's a public relations man and he has to think about that. But it's not gambling. The worst thing is a football player who bets on games."

On April 14 I met with Pete Rozelle in New York and he told me he was allowing me to remain in football. I felt as if the weight of the world had been lifted from my shoulders. As I walked out of his offices, I was as happy as a man walking out of prison, getting his first taste of freedom after a lengthy confinement. The past four months had been a series of low points, and they had taken their toll. But one thing was now certain: I had just taken my first, and most important, step on the road back.

Then, on May 19, I took a second step: I was traded to the Los Angeles Rams in a three-way deal with San Diego, and the Cowboys got another receiver named Lance. Alworth.

I was, of course, pleased and grateful. I was also despondent about leaving the Cowboys. This became very apparent to me at a huge team party held in Dallas a few days later. Almost everyone was there, part of the year-round program that Schramm and Landry had initiated to keep the players in shape and unified, part of their extraordinary capacity for total organization. The party itself was another very moving experience for me. Even though I was no longer a teammate, I had to go, to see everyone once more.

It was the first time I'd been with them since I left the meeting room in December. They were genuinely glad to see me and sorry that I'd been traded. Each player came over when no one else was around and wished me the best of luck. Many said they hoped that I would have a great day when the Rams played in Dallas. It actually didn't matter what they said, it was the way in which they said it. I could tell that I had been blessed with some true friends, and the idea of leaving them after all we had been through hurt me. At one point I really couldn't cope with my emotion and left the groups at their tables and withdrew to the relative privacy of the bar.

I don't know if I'm more sentimental than most football players. I rather doubt it. I might even be less so, since I wasn't the type to confine my social life to their world, and I probably had more outside interests than anyone on the club. It may even be an adolescent trait, this devotion to a team. What the hell is a team? you ask yourself. It's forty guys and a dozen coaches and trainers, and they're no different from the forty guys on any other club in the league. It's impossible to get very close with more than a few, certainly not in any social sense, and you don't have time to really get to know many of them, especially the guys who play different positions. But when you're working hard for a common goal, hurting and fighting, rejoicing in victory and dying in those defeats, there's a unity and comradery that develops that far transcends rivalries and any differences in personality. You learn to suffer for each other, and a tremendous sense of family comes out of it, as strong as a man's real family. At this party, then, I had to confront all those emotions, knowing that I had lost my chance to stay with them, and the fact that they still cared about me only made it all seem that much more painful. I thought then how important it was for me to find out what my problems were—and cure them.

Tom Landry would sum up those years in his own way:

Lance was an exceptionally gifted athlete and contributed greatly to the success we enjoyed. He possessed a very keen mind and always prepared himself mentally for the job that had to be done on Sunday. He set very high standards for himself and tended to become frustrated with himself when he did not reach them. He had a great need for recognition and was very sensitive to how others regarded him. He possessed the ability to read what others were thinking; however, his sensitivity at times caused him to misinterpret the thoughts of coaches and teammates, and this caused him to suffer unduly.

At times, some of his habits distracted from his concientious effort to be a good teammate. Specifically, his habit of being last to meetings and practices when everyone else was in position and ready to go, leading many of his teammates to sometimes question his dedication. We discussed his problems and frustrations at different times. When he was upset, his playing efficiency dropped off drastically. I knew there were times when he misread my thinking toward him and he would become very upset in a quiet moody manner. As soon as we would talk the air would clear and he would become his effective self again. . . . When I made the decision to trade him to Los Angeles, I was confident that this was best for Lance.

He would have the opportunity to start fresh while seeking professional help for his problems at the same time.

My prayer for Lance is that he will be able to enjoy the greatest victory of all: his own peace of mind.

I will never forget being part of this team. I will never forget the way I felt when I left them.

A few days after I was traded, columnist Dick Young blasted me again. The Los Angeles press, however, was wonderfully supportive. The Rams management was extremely happy about the trade, and their new coach, Tommy Prothro, let me know that he expected much from me. Sid Gittler negotiated an excellent contract, as good as any receiver in football, and to reinforce my exuberant feeling about my future, I went out and bought a house high in the hills above Hollywood.

On our first night out, Joey and I went to dinner at a place called Figaro's. As I came out of the men's room I heard a waiter sounding off to a table full of customers: "Yes, sir, this is a great old town. We have Joey Heatherton appearing live on stage and we have Lance Rentzel in the men's room flashing his cock."

They all roared with laughter, of course.

Welcome to Los Angeles.

XX

However, I immediately felt at home in Los Angeles. Many times I'd be walking down the street and somebody would stop his car and wish me good luck in Los Angeles. One night Jack Lemmon came over to me, introduced himself, and told me that he thought I was going to take the Rams all the way to the Super Bowl. I thought, hell, I should be introducing myself to *him*. It's the kind of thing that can lift a man's spirits considerably, and that's just what I needed.

In three weeks I was back to my normal weight, my color had returned, and my hair was longer. But more importantly, I was in better condition than ever. I went to Dallas and, while I was there, challenged Chris to a rematch of that race we had had a couple of months before.

All he saw was my heels.

When I reported to training camp, the management and the coaches went out of their way to see that everything was all right. All of the players came up and introduced themselves, a number of them saying I was the one thing they had needed to win a championship. Whether it was true or not, it made me feel great. But the comment I remember most was Marlin McKeever, an excellent middle linebacker, recalling how he'd clotheslined me a year before, and I'd gotten up off the ground and told him off. "I was real impressed by that, Lance—it takes guts for a receiver to tell a linebacker to go fuck himself."

It was Tommy Prothro's first year as a coach in the pros, and everyone wondered what he'd be like. The Rams had been led by George Allen for years, a man with a ferocious drive to win, a real slave driver. Allen was now coaching the Washington Redskins, but his presence was still felt. After a while, I'd heard so much about him I felt as though I'd played for him myself. Allen was a coach who believed in defense. I was told he would openly treat his defensive players like kings, while the offensive team sometimes wondered if they were still part of the club. But he worked everyone hard, on the field and in the meeting rooms. He never gave them a day off, telling them they could get all their rest and relaxation when they slept.

One day they lay down at practice at a prearranged signal, not saying a word. He yelled at them to get up, but they didn't move. After about ten minutes, he got the message. He told them they could do anything they wanted that night—as long as they were back in their rooms by 10:30 P.M. That wasn't much, but they figured it was the best they could do, so they got up and finished practice. After a while, many of the Rams questioned his sincerity. They began to feel that he would do anything to win. But still, he won, and they liked being winners; that was the name of the game.

Prothro, then, a mystery man to everyone, was obviously on the spot, and he chose the opposite approach. He didn't overwork us, meetings were short, we didn't even have a curfew! Preseason games were not going to be treated like the play-offs, they were going to be used mainly for evaluating the rookies. Prothro wanted us to reach a peak near the end of the season, when Allen's teams had usually gotten stale.

I believe everyone on the club liked this low-key way of doing things. We were being treated like men instead of children.

I enjoyed myself thoroughly, not only because of Prothro's relaxed atmosphere, but because I was so glad to be playing football again. It seemed like years since I had walked off that field in Dallas after the Green Bay game. I realized that I had taken things for granted before, that professional football offered a wonderful experience that would last me a lifetime. The game had been good to me, and I owed practically everything to it. Now I was getting another chance. I was back, and believe me, I was grateful.

One of the first things Prothro did was to arrange for me to get psychiatric treatment. He consulted the dean of the UCLA Medical School. They persuaded Dr. L. J. West, chief psychiatrist there, to take care of me himself. It was only after seeing Dr. West for several months that I learned that he had lived in Oklahoma City during my years there. His children had also gone to Casady. He'd seem me play football in high school and college. Furthermore, his wife had been the Casady School psychologist and knew all about me.

During the last week in July, I found out that doctors had discovered a congenital defect in Chris's heart, and he had to have open heart surgery right away. It was a stunning blow. I left for Dallas immediately, where the whole family had gathered. It seemed almost impossible to believe. He was quite a person, sincere, very mature, responsible, with an unusually fine code of ethics. He was elected to Phi Beta Kappa and had been selected as the outstanding senior man at Southern Methodist University. He had everything to live for, and yet he was facing death at twenty-one years of age.

He was taking it pretty well until he left for the hospital. But we could tell the whole thing was beginning to hit him. We attempted to reassure him, but it wasn't doing much good. So Del and I tried to make him laugh.

"Chris, can I have your car if you don't make it? I've always liked sports cars," I asked.

Then Del chimed in with, "Well, if he gets the car, will you give me your clothes? You wouldn't want your older brother to be poorly dressed, would you?"

Chris broke up. So we kept it up, and all of us were enjoying ourselves so much, we forgot what he was about to go through. As I sat there, I realized how much I loved my two brothers. All of their lives, they had lived in my shadow, a very difficult thing to cope with sometimes, but never once did they feel any resentment toward me, they were always proud and happy for me when things went well. And when I fell from grace, they shared that sorrow with me, too. It seemed ironic, considering our backgrounds, that they would turn out so well and I would have an incomprehensible emotional problem.

We left the hospital when visiting hours were over, and we returned the next morning just before he was to go into surgery. It was not the time for laughter now. Chris knew it could very well be the last time he saw us, and he gave us a letter to read in case he didn't make it. Then the nurses came and wheeled him out of the room. We all sat there, trying to show each other how confident we were that everything would be all right. But it wasn't long before Mom broke down, and we all joined her. The family had just gotten out of one crisis, and it was already in another one, even more serious. It was more than we could bear.

However, the doctors came in a couple of hours later and told us the operation was successful, and Chris was doing fine. We went up to the intensive care room and were shocked at how bad he looked. He was about to struggle through an extremely painful recovery, but he was alive, and that was all that mattered.

The L.A. Rams opened up our exhibition season against the Houston Oilers in the Hall of Fame game in Canton, Ohio. As I put on my uniform, I wondered what the fans' reaction would be. This was my first time in front of a crowd since the publicity, and I envisioned anything from cheers to insults. Before we went out for our warm-ups, Merlin Olsen came up to me and said, "Just remember, if anyone gets on you, everybody on the Rams is on your side. If you need any help, we'll be there."

When the offensive team was introduced, I got a good round of applause, which was gratifying. Of course, there were a number of people who yelled things at me, calling me the usual names like "pervert" and "fag," and needling me about my hair. But I was satisfied. It seemed the majority of people were on my side, and that's all I could ask for.

At half time Norm Van Brocklin was inducted into the Professional Football Hall of Fame. I hadn't seen him in years, so I ran up to him as the car he was in paused on its way out of the stadium.

"Hi, Norm. Congratulations on your selection. I'm really happy for you."

"What's this shit, Joe College?" he asked as he grabbed the back of my hair.

Before I could answer, the car drove off, and Van Brocklin looked back at me, laughing.

He's unbelievable.

All in all, we were a troubled team that summer, lacking confidence in our coaches as well as in ourselves. We had a poor preseason, losing more games than we won and looking bad in the process. Although the emphasis hadn't been on winning, it still bothered us. A big part of the reason for our performance was an unusual amount of injuries, mostly on artificial turf during road games. The main problem with these surfaces is their hardness. I don't know many players who like synthetic turf, especially guys who carry the ball, because when you hit the ground, it really hurts.

"Well, they're improving it," Prothro drawled. "Maybe in ten years it'll be as good as grass."

We seemed to move through the summer waiting for Prothro to make a big move that would turn everyone on. It never happened. That tentative feeling-out period just kept going on, and suddenly the season was about to begin and we were still feeling each other out. We held a few team meetings, no coaches present, just players, and we all sounded off our protests, mostly petty, but nonetheless irritating. Adjustments were made, but in the end, Prothro was the boss and we were going to play football the way he wanted us to.

I was concerned, but I recognized that Prothro's outstanding college coaching record was no accident. And besides, it wasn't really his fault. It was his first year in the

NFL, and the same went for almost every member of his coaching staff. It would take time for them to adjust to the pros, we all knew that, and after all, the preseason games don't mean that much. As Prothro said, "In December, they'll have forgotten what happened in August."

Nevertheless, it still bothered me, because I desperately needed to have a good season. If the others could afford a waiting game, I couldn't. Too many eyes would be watching me. Too many people would be all too ready to put the bad word on me if I wasn't better than ever. To play for a team that wins ball games tends to cover a multitude of sins, relieving the pressures enormously. The opposite simply reverses the pattern. I had to play well, and I had to be with a winner.

I remember telling this to Dr. West. He felt as I did, that it was enormously important that I have a good season. Somehow the way he worked with me gave me hope that things would work out.

My relationship with Joey was more open and honest than it had ever been before. Yet for the most part, it was the same. We still had fights, we still made up, and we still loved each other. And I was still trying very hard to make the marriage work. She went back to Las Vegas while I was in training camp, and I visited her when we had some time off. A day here, two days there. Once I took Roman Gabriel and his fiancée, and we had a fine time. It was always a treat for me to see Joey's act, to enjoy how entertaining a performer she was.

But it was a nervous time between us. And it didn't help matters any when Rona Barrett, a TV personality with a penchant for creating gossip out of misinformation, told the world that Joey was back together with her old boyfriend, while I was somewhere in a mental institution.

When we went to Boston to play the Patriots, I didn't talk to Joey for a couple of days. When I spoke to her again, she was in New York, and the tone of her voice told me something was wrong. I asked her what the matter was, and she told me she wanted a divorce. I said that I wouldn't stand in her way if that was what she wanted, but I asked her to reconsider. I didn't stay on the phone trying to talk her out of it. I figured the best thing to do was to try and forget it as much as possible by concerning myself with our opening game against the Saints.

Then, the day before the Rams left for New Orleans, I read about it in the papers, heard about it on the radio, saw it on TV.

The papers were filed on September 17, and the news spread around the country quickly. In every instance, naturally, my arrest was mentioned, making it appear to be the reason for the divorce. I couldn't help thinking that this was the seventh time I had received national publicity about my troubles, and I was getting weary of it. And, of course, the news wasn't complete until I found out what my friends at the *Oklahoma City Times* and the *Oklahoma Journal* had to say. They ran bold headlines on the top of the front page, above the masthead, with accompanying full-page spreads telling the "real story" behind the breakup. But the *Oklahoma Journal* had the most clever headline: "JOEY SIDELINES LANCE!"

The next day we left for the season opener, with Lance Rentzel cast in the role of Pagliacci. I knew I was going to try twice as hard to play a good game. A couple of teammates came up on the plane, wanting to know if the news was true, and I nodded. They said they were sorry, then kept glancing at me to see if I was OK. Of course I was OK.

I just felt like doing a swan dive off the wing, that was all.

On Sunday we went out there and played the worst first half in the history of the Los Angeles Rams, or so it was later written. We were behind 17-3, but Gabe rallied like a fighter coming off the floor in the late rounds. We moved ahead 20-17 with two minutes left, only to lose the game in the last three seconds when they fumbled the ball over the goal for a touchdown. A very questionable score.

But we had beaten ourselves, and when you do that, you really suffer. I had been open consistently, but the timing between Roman and me wasn't as good as it should have been, and I didn't catch that many passes. I sat alone on the plane coming home, letting my mind take me through all sorts of miserable gyrations. I worried about what kind of year I was going to have and what kind of year the Rams were going to have. We should have won easily, and I feared that this game would come back to haunt us in December when we really needed it. But most of all, I worried about Joey leaving me. She had been a vital part of my life, and now she was gone. I sipped a Coke and stared out the window into the darkness, wondering how I was going to pull myself up again.

Then, at the L.A. airport, the girl friends and wives were all there to meet the rest of the players, while I drove home by myself. I guess I was feeling pretty sorry for myself. I watched television for a couple of hours and went to bed. My body was aching, more than it usually did after a game, and that, too, bothered me. Was I getting old, as well?

Early the next morning I was awakened by a phone call.

"Hello," I said—into the wrong end of the phone.

"Lance?" It was a woman, but she was speaking into my mouth so I couldn't tell who it was.

I switched the receiver and started all over.

"Hello?"

"Lance?"

It was Joey.

"Yeah?"

"Hi," she said.

I thought, well, what now?

"Can I come over?" she asked.

She was there in twenty minutes. She moved back in that day, just as though nothing had happened. She didn't talk about the divorce, and I didn't bring it up. But her return obviously meant she still loved me, and that was all I needed to know.

And I still loved her, there was no doubt about that.

XXI

When I went on TV on the *Virginia Graham Show,* she introduced me with a beautiful play on words: "And here is Lance Rentzel, who is ramming it with the Rams!" I didn't know exactly how to take that. Not long afterward, I received a obscene cartoon in the mail, the classic one about a guy with his pants down, this time exposing himself to some mannequins in a dress shop window. There was also a long letter from a strange guy at Stanford University saying that "you are just going to have to live with the fact that you are a homosexual—which is really the nub of your problem—you simply refuse to accept that, Lance."

Then, one night, I went out to dinner with Joey, and as we walked to our table some guy recognized me, nudged his girl friend, then made the usual masturbatory gestures. I stopped, looked him right in the face, and said, "Terrific! A terrific impersonation! I knew it was me immediately!" He was really embarrassed, and I sat down thinking, Jesus, another shitty little victory.

But in general, the fans in Los Angeles were great to me, and the press treated me extremely fairly. And most important, the Rams started to win. What's more, I began to play good football for them. We beat Chicago in the last quarter on my flanker reverse. It was my first big play with the club, and the reporters gathered around my locker after the game, asking questions, and I answered with my foot in my mouth: "It was a good time to call the play. We really caught them with their pants down."

"How's that, Lance?" somebody asked, grinning from ear to ear.

"Yeah. You'd better strike that remark," I said.

Football is a game of hitting, but when the Rams and 49ers play, it's all-out war. From what I had heard about the coming game, you hope for survival as well as victory. This was apparent early in the game when Roman Gabriel suffered a concussion, and several fights almost broke out. As the first quarter ended, Jimmy Johnson—the best cornerback I've ever played against—and I had a little scuffle, but it lasted only a few seconds. A few plays later, the other cornerback, Bruce Taylor, clotheslined me brutally, knocking me on my ass, and the officials called a fifteen-yard penalty.

Immediately I saw it as a test of my ability to keep my poise, while at the same time trying to make him lose his. I started to hit him back every chance I could, especially when he played me up close in a bump-and-run coverage. I always had the advantage because I knew where the play was going and he didn't, having to turn his back to the ball to watch me. So when a run was coming my way, I lined up against Taylor and began taunting him; soon I made him so furious, he concentrated only on hitting me. Thus, in the second quarter, he didn't see Les Josephson as he cut out to the sidelines, running fifty-eight yards to set up our first touchdown. In the last quarter we were losing 13-10, and had third and one on our own thirty-six. We had an off-tackle play called to Taylor's side, a routine short-yardage call, but usually good for a couple of yards.

"Can't you hit any harder, Bruce?" I baited him.

"Watch," he said.

I could see he was really steaming—which was exactly what I wanted. Larry Smith broke into the secondary untouched, while Taylor and I were going at each other, and again he failed to see the runner. Larry ran sixty-four yards to a touchdown, putting us ahead.

By this time, everyone was watching Bruce and me as much as they were watching the rest of the game. The isolated TV cameras were following us all over the field. With a few minutes left to play, Taylor was penalized again, this time for hitting me after the whistle had blown. This gave us a first down in a crucial situation.

"Way to keep your poise," I mocked him as the official paced off fifteen big ones. It was a victory for me, although I realized I had had to learn the same lesson myself playing against Herb Adderley several years before. I didn't want to overdo it. Hell, he could very well get the best of me the next time we met.

After the game, I went up to him. "Nice game," I said, extending my hand. He wouldn't shake. "Hey, I mean it. There's no reason to have hard feelings. Let's forget about it."

"Goddamn faggot!" he snapped. "Meet me outside the locker room, and we'll see how tough you really are."

"Just check the scoreboard, Bruce," I said as I walked away.

We won, 20-13.

The Rams and the 49ers traded the division lead back and forth. Midway through the season, we were leading our conference. Two weeks later, we were one and a half games behind. It was that kind of year.

I had my first outstanding game against the Lions when I beat Dick LeBeau for two key touchdowns. There was a good reason for that: Dick Vermeil, our head offensive coach, had noticed in films that LeBeau tipped off the type of defense he was playing by his stance: when he was staring intently at the receiver in front of him, one foot forward, their secondary was going to be in a man-to-man pass defense. When his feet were even and he played slightly deeper, they were going into a zone defense. That gave us a tremendous advantage, and Gabe and I put it to good use.

After the game, the captains awarded me the game ball. That really made me feel fantastic. There is never anything so rewarding as when you win the respect of your teammates. And the 49ers lost, making the victory even sweeter.

On the following Sunday we beat San Francisco for the third straight time, 17-6, and we were back in the lead. It was once again owing primarily to the Ram defense, which had held them to one touchdown in the last two games.

And someone must have had a talk with Bruce Taylor. He didn't say a word to me.

By this time, I'd had enough time to see what the general attitude of the public was, at least as far as the sports fan was concerned. Almost all of the ridicule directed toward me came on road trips, and it was far worse in the East, particularly Baltimore. When I left the field at half time, about twenty-five men crowded around the entrance to the dressing room and hurled insults at me as I approached, threatening to back their words up with some action.

But the majority of fans treated me with compassion, and I appreciated that.

Then came the Thanksgiving encounter in Dallas, exactly one year to the day since I had played my last game for the Cowboys. The press called it my homecoming. It obviously had all kinds of significance for me. I had thought about them many times and followed their season with weekly reports from Chris, who was now almost fully recovered from his operation.

I looked forward to seeing my friends again, but I wondered what it would be like playing against them in a crucial game, where each side needed to win to stay in first place in its respective division. I also wondered how the fans would react, and I had a hundred other petty questions that mattered a great deal only to me. But I thought most about how badly I wanted to beat Dallas, like any other player who returns to meet his old club for the first time.

The Cowboys had built a brand-new $30,000,000 stadium, partially domed, with the hardest artificial turf in all of football. What made it even worse was that it had rained that week, and the field retained the moisture so thoroughly that even a helicopter could not fan it dry.

It was like playing on slippery concrete.

Merlin Olsen said, "They should take Clint Murchison up in that helicopter and drop him on this field from twenty feet up and see if he lives."

245

"If he does, I'll play on it," I replied.

All of the Cowboys called over their greetings during the warm-ups. I saw my old number, nineteen, and it was strange, I had this eerie feeling that I was seeing myself. "Hey, Lance," I hollered at Alworth. "Where'd you get the number?" He laughed.

Often during the game, when I lined up against Herb Adderley, he would make jokes after the play ended. It was a far cry from the dogfights we used to have. Once Mel Renfro came across the backfield and knocked the hell out of me when I wasn't looking. "I can really take a blow, can't I?" I said. "I already knew that," he said, smiling. Another time, I made a good catch, put on some good moves, and made a long gain. When I got near their bench, Craig was watching from close by and I could see that he was happy for me, even though it set up a touchdown for us.

We pushed the Cowboys all over the field, offensively, but we lost three fumbles, and the game, 28–21. Another of those depressing defeats that make you want to die.

I had Thanksgiving dinner at my parents' home. The whole family was there, just like the year before. At first the mood was somber because of the game; everyone had wanted me to win this one badly. And then the mood turned more serious, because Mom brought up the Adams family, and how unfair they had been to me. I sat there, thinking about the unusual parallels between the two family get-togethers. For a while everybody looked just as sad as they had the previous year.

This upset me. "Look, as far as I'm concerned, this mess is over with," I said. "I know you are only trying to support me as any loving parent would, but it's not good to carry vindictive feelings around inside of you. Just remember that things are far better for me today than they were last Thanksgiving. Not only because I'm back in football, Mom, but also because the whole affair has made me a stronger person. It didn't destroy me. I have a lot to be grateful for, beginning with my family, and I think we all should feel the same way."

She shook her head sadly. "I'm grateful for my family, too, but I won't ever forget it, not until I die."

Once again I saw how difficult it was going to be for her or Dad to forget the past. But the subject of our conversation changed, and we all snapped out of our gloom.

All things considered, it was a much better Thanksgiving than the one before.

For the Rams, the key game of the year was against George Allen's Redskins. It was vital for three reasons. First, our whole season hung in the balance on its outcome. If we won, we were almost assured of a place in the play-offs; if we lost, we were probably through. The Redskins were in the same spot. Second, it was a grudge match between George Allen and the Rams management, who had fired him after the 1970 season. So this encounter was made to appear symbolic as to who was the better coach, Prothro or Allen. Third, the Redskins had ten former Rams on their squad, eager to prove that they were on the best club. We were just as eager to prove they weren't.

Therefore it's easy to see why this had become a classic confrontation. There was far more riding on it than a possible trip to the Super Bowl. The entire city was caught up in the emotion, and a quarter of a million tickets could have been sold if the Coliseum had been large enough. It was the most important game in the Rams' history.

When a whole city the size of Los Angeles becomes

passionately involved in something that you're a part of, you have to be influenced by it. So it was with our team. All of our players had been pointing toward this game since training camp. Gabriel was more determined than I'd ever seen him.

As the kickoff drew nearer, I realized that I had been affected too. I looked upon this as the biggest game of my life, bigger than the NFL Championship against Green Bay, bigger than the Thanksgiving match with Dallas. I wanted to beat Allen and the Redskins more than anything; it began to dominate my thoughts completely.

I figured our chances were excellent. We had been through one of the toughest schedules in football, and it had molded us into a very strong club. Prothro had proved himself as a pro coach in his first year, taking a squad that had undergone radical personnel and coaching changes and making it into a winner. We had gradually developed faith in ourselves, and at this point we felt we could beat anyone, especially Washington.

Prothro had a unique approach to a significant game. He would work us less instead of more, frequently canceling one of the practices. He wanted us to be fresh. It was another contrast to Allen, who drilled his players much longer before a key game. As a matter of fact, everything about Protho was the opposite of Allen, and considering the circumstances in which he came to the Rams, I guess it was planned that way.

We met the Redskins on Monday night, in front of a national television audience. Before the pre-game warmups, I sensed we were ready. Too ready. In fact, we were very tight, and that can be bad. It can cause you to play poorly, without that touch of reckless abandon, because you're afraid to make a mistake. I understood why we were in that frame of mind; all week long the coaches had told us we would win if we didn't make any big errors, that Washington's style of play was to force mistakes, and then take advantage of them. And the coaches were right: the best way to beat them was not to beat ourselves.

But we had become too conscious of that strategy, and too aware of the importance of the struggle that was about to take place, resulting in our being extremely tense. This wasn't good, and I was worried about it, especially since I saw the same signs in myself. I always approach a game with a somewhat casual attitude, and I perform best when I am relaxed. But I could feel the tension inside me, and I didn't like it.

I rarely say anything when everyone gathers in the locker room just before leaving for the kickoff. I think there are too many speeches. But this time I said something, I felt my words might help the team—and myself.

"We can take them if we play our game. Let's not worry about making a mistake so much that we're too tight. All we have to do is stay loose, and keep our poise. We'll win if we keep our poise. . . ."

I then proceeded to play the worst game of my life, making all sorts of dumb mistakes and, worst of all, losing my poise. For the first time all year, opposing players hurled insults at me from the bench: "Flasher . . . Hollywood fag . . . pervert," and other such names. It surprised me, although I knew immediately that they were trying to get my goat, looking for anything that would give them an edge. I tried to ignore them, but the name-calling continued. I don't know if it affected my playing or not—but if it did, it shouldn't have. I do know I dropped several passes and played very poorly in general. We lost, and I felt that I was a big factor in the defeat.

As George Allen was walking to the locker room, he noticed that he was right behind a number of the Ram front office personnel. He couldn't resist.

"It's sweet to win," he said. When he got no response, he repeated it.

"It's really sweet to win." Again, no comment.

"I mean it. Some guys just don't know how sweet it is to win."

I was close by, I heard everything, and it made the loss even more difficult for me to take.

I told myself not to make any more little speeches.

The season ended with an anticlimactic victory in Pittsburgh. That week was a miserable one for me. It started out with two automobile accidents on successive days, both of which caused me to be late for practice. That cost me $250 in fines. The week ended in Pittsburgh, where I received a few malicious phone calls in the hotel, topped off with a near fight with a group of antagonistic fans who surrounded me as I tried to leave the stadium.

It was a great way to finish the season.

I was tired, more tired than I'd ever been after the last game. Nineteen seventy-one had been a very long year with enough turbulence to last any man a lifetime. I'd been through a felony case, almost a banishment from my profession, humiliating publicity, an uprooting trade, a divorce filing, and through it all, a fight to reestablish myself on what I'd like to think of as a comeback. Sure, I was tired. I sat in that locker room with my uniform on far longer than usual, and when I went into the shower, there were very few guys left. I saw Dick Vermeil, the offensive coach, and though the shower water was pouring all over him, I could see he was crying. I knew how he felt. An exhausted, beaten-down loss of control. You put out all that effort, all that emotion; in the end, you feel drained, especially if you don't come home with all the marbles. I didn't say anything to him. There was really nothing to say.

During the plane ride back to Los Angeles, I reflected on my first year with the Rams. It had been a good season, but not a great one. My main problem had been perfecting my timing with Roman Gabriel. But I had every reason to believe that this would come with more work together. And the team had every reason to expect a definite improvement for next season—all of us, coaches and players alike, were getting to know each other better. That can make a big difference.

Everyone connected with the Ram organization had gone out of his way to make me feel welcome, and I felt I was very much a part of this team; in fact, I felt I was very much a part of Los Angeles.

Tommy Prothro: *"A football player has to be respected for his contribution to the team. That is foremost. I've seen fine gentlemen who fouled up on the field and upset a team by the way they played. Everything else about them, all those fine gentlemanly qualities, were relatively meaningless as a result. A good football player is a lot more important to a team than a fine gentleman. Lance was respected for his abilities. Then, because of his personality, he became well liked, too."*

Roman Gabriel: *"I really didn't care about Lance's reputation, all I cared about was whether he was a good receiver. Football players don't give much of a damn what a guy does off the field . . . that's his business. . . ."*

251

It had taken me a long time to realize that. Catch the football and whatever else you do is more or less irrelevant—except to yourself. For too long I had been overly concerned about the approval of others and had never faced up to what I was to myself. In Dallas I had been shocked into realizing how destructive that lack of self-scrutiny was. The whole affair could turn out to be a blessing in disguise, for it forced me to seek a new level of self-understanding.

Now I am working hard on myself, as hard as I have ever worked on a football field. My problems are far more mysterious than I thought they would be. There has proved to be no single childhood incident or traumatic experience to explain my problems. The causes and effects are subtle, probably involving relationships more than events. Much of this still lies buried somewhere deep in my subconscious.

The first thing I had to admit to myself was that I really had an emotional problem. I had always denied that before. Once I faced that openly, I began to make some progress. Then one day Dr. West asked me if I would be willing to speak to a class of medical students at UCLA, to describe myself and something of my case history. For the first time in my life I said it right out loud to a hundred strangers: "Ladies and gentlemen, by medical definition, I am a sex pervert." For a twenty-eight-year-old golden boy whose whole life had been devoted to living up to his image, that was one hell of an achievement.

In my first year of self-examination, I have not yet come up with a complete explanation of my problem, but there have been more than a few helpful insights. These have come from being forced to look into myself, to dig out what my inner conflicts are. Exhibitionism is not my whole problem; it is probably the most obvious symptom of it, the tip of the iceberg. To find out more, I had to go back to early childhood, to complex and obscure emotional currents and countercurrents in the life of my family, especially in my relations with my parents, and their relations with each other.

Many of the conflicts beneath the surface of my family life were not unusual, but certain relationships were perhaps out of balance: for example, a mother who was highly affectionate and perhaps overconcerned with me, and a father who was a powerful person but a somewhat remote figure because of his extensive travels.

This unusual intimacy with an intensely devoted mother threatened me. Subconsciously perhaps, she didn't want her children to grow up, but her preoccupation with me could also have been conditioned by my older brother's frailty and illness. I do know that I tried to resolve this ambivalence toward my mother by escaping from her, by pursuing a supermasculine image to prove to myself that I wouldn't always be a baby. In doing so, I also removed any fear of reprisal from my father; he simply had to approve of me if I excelled in all the ways that I felt were important to him. So I became a Superboy, who would presumably grow into a Superman. I did all the approved things: earned good grades in school, starred in athletics, and won the most beautiful girls.

However, two emotionally immature patterns developed out of this. One was the need to prove my masculinity over and over. The other was an inability to establish a permanent, meaningful adult relationship with a woman. How could I allow myself to get that close to a woman? She would smother me, as I felt my mother did, and then I couldn't be a man.

As I grew older, these conflicts resulted in a number of unconscious defenses for my emotional protection. They included a constant need for female conquests, a compulsion to be vigorously and continually active, and a demanding competitive drive to be a winner.

However, at various times in my life, these defenses failed me. This happened when I could no longer repress the anxiety welling up from the conflicts within me, owing to a number of pressures building up at once, while at the same time I felt no reassurance in the Superman department, because I was losing instead of winning. I felt defeated, emasculated. At that point there would arise the necessity to resort to a very childish gesture to prove my masculinity: self-exposure. It derived from a feeling of power and excitement that had come from an accidental but sexually meaningful episode of exposure when I was around twelve years old, with a girl about the same age.

In exposing myself as an adult, I was a half-grown boy again, reverting in search of a gesture that would reassure me that I was, in fact, not emasculated after all. A girl the same age would symbolize that earlier incident, with all its innocence and importance; for a moment I was Superboy again, with my vital parts intact. Needless to say, there was no desire for actual contact with a female at that point. The act was more magical than sexual, a ritual to restore that all important sense of power that the defeats of life had temporarily destroyed.

I had not experienced this childish impulse very often. After the second time I got caught, however, I was forced to stop and take a look at myself. This led directly to the process of self-exploration in which I am still engaged. Once I was able to start asking some questions, I finally began to arrive at some answers.

One of the first areas I examined was my marriage to Joey. I had realized before that our difficulties were mutual, but I began to see the deep-seated conflicts inside me that aggravated our troubles. Sometimes Joey used to

254

call me "a man's man." On the surface this could be related to some insensitivity on my part, or a preference for masculine pursuits over those of family life. However, I now believe what she was sensing was my subconscious fear of letting her get too close to me. Joey misinterpreted this as a lack of love for her. Most of our misunderstandings began there, fed by her own doubts about marriage.

I loved Joey so much that she was able to break through the barrier that I had put up against all women. However, the old conflicts in my subconscious were not so easy for me to be rid of. I could not keep from holding myself apart from her at times. She naturally wanted to be as close as possible to me, but I resisted that, still unconsciously afraid of what might happen if I didn't keep my distance: that I'd be reduced to a momma's boy.

One trouble was that I had become an expert at repressing any emotions that threatened me. I could hide things about myself that I didn't want to see and thus could avoid untoward feelings. This is a good quality to have on the football field. It has enabled me to concentrate completely on catching the ball, repressing the fear of getting hit or dropping it. Under normal conditions this overdeveloped ability to repress allowed me to go through a full game without emotional interference or distraction. Well, that was fine when I was playing football, but it's no way to spend your whole life. Football was—and is—very important to me; but life isn't football, and football is only one part of the life of even the most devoted player.

In treatment, the questions about myself go on and on. The more I learn to answer some of them, the more others appear. Yet patterns emerge; gradually I've come to know enough about myself to face these revelations, no matter how painful or unflattering they may be. I have made progress. I am better able to believe that I am a man without continually having to prove it. At least I have had no further impulses toward exposing myself. There is no reason for me to fear closeness with a woman; now that I understand that, perhaps I can make a more profound commitment to a woman. Maybe I can learn to open up more and not be afraid to let myself know in truth what I feel.

No matter that I'm still trying to figure out what life is all about. I still ponder on the nature of God and humanity and what makes us all the way we are. I've had the opportunity, as a result of what has happened to me, to see some of the good and bad sides of human nature, and it's made me much more appreciative of what I am and what I can be. It is only through admitting weakness that one can become strong, and this, too, I have learned. In a way, it is the basis for this book.

So it is that a guy like me can begin to grow up before it's too late. My parents aren't to be blamed for my flaws. They are guilty of only loving me as much as they could in the best ways that they could. Particularly my mother. I have come to realize that in the past I had misinterpreted most of her actions. She was only trying to give her children the things she had never had as a child, and I appreciate that. Many kids have to grow up with a mother who doesn't care at all.

I believe this experience has benefited the whole family in one way. We have become closer than ever and will remain so, no matter how far apart we are living and how much our interests vary. That thought alone is like the light at the end of a tunnel.

For reasons of sentiment, I suppose, I found myself as a spectator at the Super Bowl in January, 1972. Once again the Cowboys had come up off the ground and made it there—without me. Again I did not visit them at practice, but I rejoiced at their overwhelming victory over Miami. After all those grueling years of failure and frustration they finally went all the way. That, too, was an ending for me. It was something I still wanted for myself. I would never feel fully complete as a football player until I achieved it, and now this club that had once been mine had won the greatest prize of all. Their triumph aroused in me both exhilaration and sorrow; I could not help wishing I had been a part of it and thinking that I had only myself to blame that I wasn't.

After the game I walked out of the stadium toward the locker rooms. Even with the huge crowd gathered out in front, I could hear that wonderfully riotous celebration going on inside. I had to laugh at the picture of it in my mind. Hayes, Morton, Green, Lilly, Garrison, Staubach—all those terrific guys dousing each other with champagne. I made a move to go in and say hello, but I was stopped at the door. The cop who was guarding it asked, "Who are you?"

For a moment I stood there in silence. I could have answered him and gone inside and joined in the fun. But I didn't. Although I would always feel a special closeness to the Cowboys, they weren't my team anymore. That was another part of my life, and it was over.

I walked away, went to the airport, and flew home to Los Angeles.

An Epilogue

Louis Jolyon West, M. D.*

The achievement of manhood was the theme of Rudyard
Kipling's famous poem "If." Much of it has been quoted in
reference to war, politics, and sports. One couplet is
inscribed over the center-court entrance at Wimbledon:

> If you can meet with Triumph and Disaster
> And treat those two imposters just the same . . .

The message is that manhood is reached through a
process of inner growth; that it does not require the proofs
furnished by winning contests or battles; that it cannot be
shaken by the shocks of defeat.

*Professor and Chairman, Department of Psychiatry, UCLA; Medical
Director, the Neuropsychiatric Institute.

Kipling's poem was published more than sixty years ago. It seems old-fashioned today. Even Grantland Rice, considered by my generation to be a veritable guru in the world of sports, sounds quaint when we hear again his famous lines.

> When the One Great Scorer comes
> to write against your name—
> He marks—not that you won or lost—
> but how you played the game.

Today things are different. The contemporary athlete's shibboleth is more likely to be that attributed to the late Vince Lombardi, for many years coach of the professional football team known as the Green Bay Packers:

> Winning isn't the most important thing;
> it's the *only* thing."

The meaning of winning in football and some of the psychodynamics of players and coaches have been discussed insightfully by Dr. Chester M. Pierce, one of Harvard's all-time great football players, now a professor of psychiatry at the Harvard Medical School. To those who are interested in the problems of football players, I recommend his articles. However, while football players have all kinds of problems, both mental and physical, Lance Rentzel's story is clearly an unusual one.

The tremendous emphasis on winning is a significant characteristic of American culture today. Many youngsters rebel against it completely and turn to profoundly noncompetitive modes of life such as those in the counter-culture or the Green Rebellion. An even larger group—in fact the vast majority—of young people suffer from the national preoccupation with winning because the joys and rewards of sports are to a significant degree denied them.

Schools, clubs, YMCAs, business concerns are all obsessed with producing or sponsoring winning teams. An inordinate emphasis upon championships can easily lead to neglect of the average performer, whose life and health can nevertheless be greatly enriched by regular participation in sports. Lance Rentzel's former coach (and my old colleague) Charles B. (Bud) Wilkinson has been concerned with this problem for many years. In fact, since leaving coaching he has become president of the Lifetime Sports Foundation, which gives this idea a high priority.

It is only because of a minor quirk in Lance Rentzel's sexual maturation that the exaggerated importance he places on winning has come to his attention. Exhibitionism is a relatively mild sexual symptom, almost a trivial one compared with other more frequent manifestations of sexual maldevelopment that rarely come to light. For example, the need to be brutal or punitive toward one's sexual partner is not an uncommon problem in the lives of professional athletes. It is not often publicized, however; even when horrendous accounts are given by girl friends or wives seeking legal redress, the press and the public take little heed. But exhibitionists are usually apprehended quickly and easily; the nature of the impulse precludes elaborate or effective precautions. Then, if the man is a celebrity, he's in big trouble.

The role of defeat or loss is often found to play a major part in the appearance of self-exposure as a symptom. It is as though the patient (nearly always a man) suddenly needs to be certain that his manhood is intact, and is impelled to demonstrate that fact to a female. Perennial exhibitionists are usually chronic losers, at least in some way meaningful to themselves. But there are many instances of men of all ages, who have never had such an impulse before in their lives, suddenly exposing themselves in public after suffering a defeat in business, or losing a significant amount of money in a bad investment, or incurring some other setback in one of life's arenas. The pitiful exhibitionism of old men is, of course, well known.

On the rare occasions when Lance Rentzel experienced the impulse to exhibit himself he was feeling like a loser. And while other elements compounded the problem, his preoccupation with being a winner as a football player was always involved. Needless to say, the tremendous focus of public attention upon star performers like Lance Rentzel, the intense scrutiny given their every move and particularly to their mistakes, serves to exaggerate the strain. The pressures generated by coaches, fans, and the media upon outstanding athletes are almost beyond the comprehension of ordinary citizens.

It goes without saying that the stress undergone by great athletes is physical as well as mental. Lance Rentzel's manuscript, except for a couple of vivid examples, underemphasizes this. He has had many injuries, including a number of severe concussions and other head injuries. Even so, because of his superb physique and quickness, he is one of the least-injured professional football players in the game.

It is most unusual for a psychiatrist to permit his relationship with a patient to become public knowledge. However, there are many unusual things about the case of Lance Rentzel. For example, he and I are required to make periodic reports on his progress to several public and private agencies. Moreover, the decision to publish this book (the writing of which I encouraged as part of the psychotherapeutic process) was made independently by him, after much deliberation. In my view Lance Rentzel's reasons for deciding to publish it were healthy ones.

It is also irregular for a psychiatrist to treat someone with whom he has had some previous relationship. Although Lance didn't know it when he was referred to

261

me, I was acquainted with his father during the years when we both lived in Oklahoma (where I was a member of the university's medical faculty). I already knew a great deal about his family and about his personal history before he first came to see me at the UCLA Medical School last summer.

Lance Rentzel was marked as a gifted child intellectually and musically before he finished second grade. Soon afterward it became evident that he was also an extraordinary physical specimen. At the age of seven he was winning contests of all kinds against ten-year-olds.

At Oklahoma City's Casady School (which my children also attended during the Rentzel era) Lance was for three straight years on the first string varsity teams in football, basketball, baseball, and track. He also excelled in tennis and golf. At the same time he was an outstanding student. In those days my wife was Assistant (for Counseling and Guidance) to the Headmaster of Casady School. It was easy for me, therefore, to obtain an objective summary of Lance Rentzel's high school record. It looked something like this:

Second in Junior Class 1960
Fifth in Senior Class 1961
Scholastic Award 1960
Mathematics Award 1961
Dartmouth Cup 1961 (awarded to Casady's best scholastic-athletic combination)
All American Prep Football Team
Little All City Back-of-the-Year
Little All City Football Team (Junior and Senior Year)
All Conference Football Team (Junior and Senior Year)
12 Varsity Letters (3 each in Football, Basketball, Baseball, and Track)

Gold Medal—Oklahoma Music Festival 1960–1961 (Piano)

All Conference Baseball Team (Junior and Senior Year)

All Conference Basketball Team 1961

Little All City Basketball Team 1961 (scored 374 points)

Little All City Baseball Team 1961 (Batting Average .427)

Casady's Most Valuable Player in Football 1961 (scored 144 points)

Casady's Most Valuable Player in Basketball 1961

Casady's Most Valuable Player Award in Track (broke Southwest Conference Broad Jump record, which still stands)

As a former faculty member of the University of Oklahoma I could easily reconstruct Lance Rentzel's record there, as well:

Selected as one of the "Top Ten Outstanding Freshman Men at University of Oklahoma" 1962

Dean's Honor List

3 Varsity Letters in Football

NEA All American

All Big Eight Halfback

Associated Press Back-of-the-Week (September, 1964)

Senior Bowl Squad 1964 (Mobile, Alabama)

College All Star Squad 1965 (Chicago)

Who's Who in American Colleges and Universities

Member O.U. Student Council

There was more to the Rentzel legend. For example, I was present at his last high school football game when, after scoring four touchdowns, and with nothing stopping him from scoring the fifth, he deliberately ran the ball out of bounds on the one-foot line, so that one of his teammates (who had never scored a touchdown) could make the final score.

My daughter, a pianist, told me of the stir occasioned when Lance Rentzel, by then an All-American football player, took the time during final examinations at the university to return and play in his former piano teacher's annual recital, thereby demonstrating to all of her younger students that taking piano lessons didn't necessarily mean you were a sissy.

Knowing all this about the young man, it was as surprising to me as it was to anyone when the Minneapolis episode was reported and when, subsequently, the much more serious scandal in Dallas burst forth upon the scene. When Coach Tommy Prothro asked me to see Lance Rentzel in consultation, after he was traded to the Los Angeles Rams, I was glad to be of help. However, it was not my intention to treat him myself; I expected to send him for psychotherapy to someone else. But the function of trust is crucial in effective psychotherapy. Lance insisted that he wanted to work with me, and in the end I agreed.

Treatment has been somewhat unorthodox (just as is the writing of this epilogue!) but, so far, it could be called reasonably successful. In large part this has been because of the patient's determination and courage. Psychotherapy isn't easy under the best of conditions; it is even harder when the commissioner, the court, the parole board, and the team management are looking over your shoulder. Lance Rentzel has never faltered in his determination to overcome the symptom that has already cost him so much, and I believe that he will succeed.

It would be inappropriate for me to discuss Lance Rentzel's treatment any further than he has already chosen to do in his manuscript. Clearly, however, it has been necessary for him to separate the meaning of winning at football from the assessment of his own value as a person. His psychiatric disorder is less an affliction than it is an impairment of maturation in a rather small area of personality. As I have known him and worked with him in the past year, it has become clear to me that Lance Rentzel is capable of—and indeed has demonstrated—continuing growth. This should stand him in good stead in many ways, including his ability to further fulfill his potentialities as a professional athlete.

Thus, what you have read by Lance Rentzel is neither a book about football nor a book about psychiatry. It is a book about growing up. Lance Rentzel has had more than his share of both Triumph and Disaster. He was not able to treat those two imposters just the same. I hope that in the future he will.

There will be no diminishing of Lance Rentzel's fierce competitiveness—that is an integral part of his character. But, through progressive self-understanding and self-acceptance, he will become more completely secure in his identity regardless of the outcome of any football game.

When you have reached that point, then you are a real winner in the larger game of life. And then, as Kipling summed it up:

Yours is the Earth and everything that's in it,
And—which is more—you'll be a Man, my son!

Los Angeles, California
June 5, 1972